Sciences

A PRACTICAL GUIDE TEACHER BOOK

Fiona Clark

David Mindorff

Rita Pak

International Baccalaureate
Baccalauréat International
Bachillerato Internacional

Sciences: A practical guide (Teacher book)

Published on behalf of the International Baccalaureate Organization, a not-for-profit educational foundation of 15 Route des Morillons, 1218 Le Grand-Saconnex, Geneva, Switzerland by the

International Baccalaureate Organization (UK) Ltd,
Peterson House, Malthouse Avenue, Cardiff Gate, Cardiff, Wales CF23 8GL
United Kingdom, represented by IB Publishing Ltd, Churchillplein 6,
The Hague, 2517JW, The Netherlands.
Website: www.ibo.org

The International Baccalaureate Organization (known as the IB) offers four high-quality and challenging educational programmes for a worldwide community of schools, aiming to create a better, more peaceful world. This publication is one of a range of materials produced to support these programmes.

British Library Cataloguing in Publication Data

A catalogue record for this book is available from the British Library

ISBN: 978-1-910160-05-3
MYP371

Printed in India

IB Publishing would like to thank Aileen Harvey and Dan Rosen for their contributions to the writing and editing of this book.

Acknowledgments

I would like to thank my family, Eric and Ayra Boonstra, for their love and support during the writing process —Rita.

The IB may use a variety of sources in its work and checks information to verify accuracy and authenticity, particularly when using community-based knowledge sources such as Wikipedia. The IB respects the principles of intellectual property and makes strenuous efforts to identify and obtain permission before publication from rights holders of all copyright material used. The IB is grateful for permissions received for material used in this publication and will be pleased to correct any errors or omissions at the earliest opportunity.

This publication may contain web addresses of websites created and maintained by other public and/or private organizations. The IB provides links to these sites for information purposes only. The presence of a link is not an IB endorsement of the site and the IB is not responsible for the content of external Internet sites. When you copy a link to an outside website(s), you are subject to the privacy and security policies of the owners/sponsors of the outside website(s). The IB is not responsible for the information collection practices of non-IB sites. You are reminded that while all web addresses referenced in this publication were correct at the time of writing, links can quickly become obsolete and we are unable to guarantee that links will continue to remain active. We apologize if you find that a particular link no longer works.

IB learner profile

The aim of all IB programmes is to develop internationally minded people who, recognizing their common humanity and shared guardianship of the planet, help to create a better and more peaceful world.

As IB learners we strive to be:

INQUIRERS
We nurture our curiosity, developing skills for inquiry and research. We know how to learn independently and with others. We learn with enthusiasm and sustain our love of learning throughout life.

KNOWLEDGEABLE
We develop and use conceptual understanding, exploring knowledge across a range of disciplines. We engage with issues and ideas that have local and global significance.

THINKERS
We use critical and creative thinking skills to analyse and take responsible action on complex problems. We exercise initiative in making reasoned, ethical decisions.

COMMUNICATORS
We express ourselves confidently and creatively in more than one language and in many ways. We collaborate effectively, listening carefully to the perspectives of other individuals and groups.

PRINCIPLED
We act with integrity and honesty, with a strong sense of fairness and justice, and with respect for the dignity and rights of people everywhere. We take responsibility for our actions and their consequences.

OPEN-MINDED
We critically appreciate our own cultures and personal histories, as well as the values and traditions of others. We seek and evaluate a range of points of view, and we are willing to grow from the experience.

CARING
We show empathy, compassion and respect. We have a commitment to service, and we act to make a positive difference in the lives of others and in the world around us.

RISK-TAKERS
We approach uncertainty with forethought and determination; we work independently and cooperatively to explore new ideas and innovative strategies. We are resourceful and resilient in the face of challenges and change.

BALANCED
We understand the importance of balancing different aspects of our lives—intellectual, physical, and emotional—to achieve well-being for ourselves and others. We recognize our interdependence with other people and with the world in which we live.

REFLECTIVE
We thoughtfully consider the world and our own ideas and experience. We work to understand our strengths and weaknesses in order to support our learning and personal development.

The IB learner profile represents 10 attributes valued by IB World Schools. We believe these attributes, and others like them, can help individuals and groups become responsible members of local, national and global communities.

International Baccalaureate®
Baccalauréat International
Bachillerato Internacional

Contents

How to use this book

The teacher book is designed both as a companion to the student book and to facilitate a whole-school approach to science skills development in Middle Years Programme students. As well as providing definitions and explanations for key concepts, this book includes supporting activities, task guidelines and assessment criteria that have been specified for the tasks.

The student and teacher books provide a detailed introduction to the key and related concepts in MYP Sciences.

The key concept chapters look at the challenges and benefits of teaching for conceptual learning and introduce science skills. Ideas for teaching these concepts and skills are provided; some of these are linked to the student book and form extensions of activities located therein, others are new activities that you can use in your classes to motivate and engage students' understanding of conceptual learning and skills development.

The related concept chapters support the delivery of the related concepts in the classroom. Teacher guidance is provided to complement the activities in the student book.

Throughout the book you will find features and teaching suggestions that will help you link your teaching to the core elements of the MYP. Here are some of the features you will come across:

DIPLOMA PROGRAMME LINKS
Opportunities to link to the DP curriculum.

INTERDISCIPLINARY LINKS
These boxes provide links to other subject groups.

CHAPTER LINKS
MYP students are encouraged to use skills and knowledge from different subject areas. These boxes link to other chapters, which relate to a topic or theme.

WEB LINKS
The student and teacher books have integrated references to Internet tools and sources in each chapter.

TEACHING IDEA
These boxes give additional ideas to the activities in the student book.

QUICK THINK
These boxes refer to the Quick Think in the student book and give further guidance on how to use these suggestions to extend student learning or to facilitate a discussion.

TIP
Throughout the chapters you will see additional tips for teaching.

☄ TAKE ACTION
This box relates to the student book and gives teaching-specific suggestions around encouraging students to use their study to contribute to the wider community and to make a difference in their own lives or the lives of others.

Introduction to IB Skills

Welcome to *IB Skills: Sciences* for MYP 4/5. This book complements the student book and aims to assist teachers in helping IB MYP students develop and apply inquiry skills in science. The inquiry-based activities are designed to enable students to approach scientific concepts through tasks set in authentic contexts that address genuine scientific problems.

These books are aimed at providing opportunities for students to learn and practise scientific skills as part of their MYP course. All of the activities are accessible for all MYP students. The open-ended nature of inquiry tasks allows teachers to differentiate each activity for the abilities of the students they teach.

MYP Sciences embodies the philosophy that being an effective scientist requires the knowledge and application of the specific skills of designing, carrying out and evaluating experiments. The student book guides the students through the MYP key and related concepts in different contexts, posing stimulating questions for reflection and opportunities for research. The teacher book provides guidance for each activity, while also providing information for unit planning, teaching ideas and opportunities for further inquiry.

It is hoped that the variety of activities across the different concepts will provide teachers with the opportunity to use the books as a unique resource, incorporating the tasks that will best serve the needs of their students, while also preparing them for further scientific studies, including the IB Diploma Programme.

Teaching the concepts

The MYP has developed a conceptual framework that includes key concepts and related concepts.

Key concepts

Each subject area in the MYP has key concepts that provide a framework for knowledge and understanding. In the sciences, there are three key concepts through which material can be approached in order to understand the natural world.

Systems are sets of interacting or interdependent components.

Change is a conversion/shift/movement from one state to another.

Relationships are the connections and associations between properties, forces, objects, people and ideas.

These key concepts are explored in detail in Chapters 2 to 4.

Related concepts

In addition to the key concepts, there are 12 related concepts, covered in Chapters 5 to 16. These 12 concepts are related to the modular sciences course, and also have significant overlap with the related concepts for biology, chemistry and physics. Through these related concepts, key subject skills and techniques are demonstrated and explained.

Related concepts for modular science		
energy	interaction	function
evidence	consequences	patterns
transformation	form	environment
models	movement	balance

In each chapter of the student book there are a variety of activities that pertain to each related concept, designed to encourage students to become effective independent learners. It is anticipated that the student and teacher books will be used in conjunction in the classroom to teach students scientific concepts and skills.

For each activity, the teacher book provides guidance notes along with teaching ideas, tips and areas for further exploration. Where appropriate, answers to questions are also provided.

While it is possible to use these books in isolation, it is certainly not required. As different chapters of the books relate to different areas of the curriculum, it is intended that teachers use each chapter, or even activity within a chapter, when they feel it is appropriate and most pertinent to the unit being studied at the time.

Assessment objectives

All MYP subjects are assessed using four criteria, each of which are designed to measure a different scientific skill and given a mark out of eight. These are:

Criterion A	Knowing and understanding
Criterion B	Inquiring and designing
Criterion C	Processing and evaluating
Criterion D	Reflecting on the impacts of science

These books focus on providing students with the skills assessed by criteria B and C. These objectives represent some of the crucial skills required by scientists.

Criterion B emphasizes inquiry through experimentation. In order to achieve the highest levels, students will need to explain problems and why they are possible to investigate scientifically, thus formulating testable hypotheses. Students are also required to explain how to design experiments to collect accurate and repeatable data as a result of manipulating variables.

Criterion C focuses on the collection and processing of data and the evaluation of the validity of experimental methods. In order to achieve the highest levels, students will need to present raw and transformed data to make accurate interpretations and explanations using scientific reasoning. Students will also need to evaluate the strengths and limitations of methods and provide explanations on how to improve or extend the experiment.

As the chapters and activities in these books focus only on criteria B and C it is possible to use them as stand-alone units or as a component of a unit that also assesses other criteria. It is expected that teachers will incorporate the activities in the best manner that suits their scheme of work.

Using the concepts to design learning

It is expected that MYP teachers will design their own units of study that incorporate their own curriculum with the philosophy of the MYP. For this, each unit will have one key concept as well as one or more related concepts.

For any topic within the sciences, it is possible to plan an MYP unit based on each of the key concepts. Along with the related concepts, it is therefore possible to teach any unit in a way that is appropriate for your class, school or country. There is no right or wrong way to approach scientific material, but by using key and related concepts it is possible to create a unique learning environment specific to the learning needs of your students. The chapters and activities in these books can therefore be studied in isolation or as part of a teacher-designed unit.

MYP unit planner

MYP Sciences is a philosophy of teaching, encouraging the development of skills and approaches to learning within the IB MYP framework. As such, there is no set curriculum or content list, but the ideas and philosophy of the MYP can be applied to any curriculum, whether it is designed by the school or prescribed by a local or national authority.

Global contexts

The focus of the MYP is to teach concepts in context. Contextualized learning helps students to apply their knowledge and understanding to the real world. There are six global contexts each with their own descriptors, which can be found in the *Sciences* curriculum guide or *Principles into practice*.

It is expected that each unit of study will specify the global context within which the material is to be learned. When planning a unit, the selection of the global context can be made before the content is chosen, but it is also possible to plan the content to be covered before selecting the appropriate context. As each unit requires at least one summative assessment, it is often simplest to select the global context based on the summative task. If the summative task easily fits one or more global contexts, then it is probably appropriate and is therefore a valuable approach to learning.

Statements of inquiry

Statements of inquiry bring together the key and related concepts with the global context, and explain what the students will be studying and why. It can be interesting for students to reflect on the statements of inquiry before and after studying the units.

Inquiry questions

Each unit is also required to have inquiry questions that enhance student learning, encouraging inquiry through questioning. Factual questions normally focus on the specific content and material to be studied that can be answered by the recall of knowledge. Conceptual questions require application of knowledge or the exploration of the ideas that connect facts together. Debatable questions encourage discussion and have no correct answer. These are often provocative and encourage evaluation of ideas.

Inquiry questions should guide students and teachers through the ideas that they should be thinking about. When incorporating the chapters and activities from these books into your units of study, synthesize inquiry questions that can be answered as a result of completing the activities. This will help students learn the skills and concepts from the book in the context of your curriculum and units.

Stage 1 of the unit planner

Where activities are appropriate for use as a summative assessment, activity guidance includes "stage 1 of the unit planner". The assessment is activity specific and the assessment criteria provided are always the task-specific descriptors for the top band (7–8) within each criterion. As these books focus on criteria B and C, possible assessment activities are restricted to these criteria.

The unit planner includes the key and related concepts, a global context and a statement of inquiry. These are designed to be a starting point for teachers to design units that can incorporate the activity as an assessment. Teachers can use these sections for stand-alone units, or incorporate the activity/assessment into existing units.

Summary

The role of an MYP Sciences teacher is to design exciting and engaging units that allow students to acquire the necessary skills to become independent learners and scientists, and the tasks that students undertake are fundamental to this. The *IB Skills: Sciences* books are not traditional textbooks that need to be followed from start to finish. They are meant to be study companions to support students while they learn inquiry skills. The activities within each chapter can be used in isolation, as part of the chapter or as entire units. It is up to teachers to decide what is in the best interest of their students.

Teaching MYP Sciences is about providing opportunities for students to learn key scientific concepts by asking questions, both of the natural world and of their own learning. By following inquiry opportunities in different contexts, students will learn a variety of fundamental scientific skills and be able to apply these skills in different contexts. The teacher book is intended to support MYP teachers in designing exciting and effective units to enable their students to become independent, life-long learners.

Introducing key concept 1: systems

	ATL skills	Science skills
Activity 1 Classifying systems	✓ Make inferences and draw conclusions.	✓ Make connections between relevant information to draw conclusions.
Activity 2 Using Kepler's laws	✓ Analyse complex concepts and projects into their constituent parts and synthesize them to create new understanding.	✓ Solve problems set in unfamiliar situations.
Activity 3 Thermoregulation	✓ Gather and organize relevant information to formulate an argument.	✓ Formulate a hypothesis and explain it using scientific reasoning.

Introducing systems

Systems are sets of interacting or interdependent components. Sciences attempt to describe both the function and interaction of these components to help us understand the underlying governing principles of science. Every branch of science and all scientific ideas are part of many systems. By investigating each system, students will be able to understand the interconnectivity of the sciences to understand the place of scientific principles in the world.

This key concept enables students to structure and order their knowledge to establish how scientific processes occur. Students often find it challenging to connect their knowledge to form meaningful ideas. By structuring their ideas into different systems, students can create models that simplify concepts by limiting variables. This can help clarify understanding of a topic and its interaction with other systems as well as enable further investigation of a particular idea.

In this chapter, students will learn to make inferences and draw conclusions about systems and their components. Students will investigate open and closed systems in conjunction with static and dynamic systems. They will learn how modification of one part of a system can directly or indirectly affect other parts of the system, or even potentially impact a totally separate system.

Activity 1 Classifying systems

In this activity, students are required to think about the movement of resources and materials into and out of a system. This helps to clarify what is and is not part of any given system. It is important that students understand the difference between matter and energy. If they do not, they will struggle to understand the difference between an open and a closed system.

Image	Type of system
Pot on stove with lid	Closed—no material can leave the pot. Only energy leaves.
Pot on stove without lid	Open—liquid can evaporate out of the pot and other substances can be added.
Insulated bottle	Closed—no material can leave. Energy can leave but very slowly.
Earth	Open—materials leave and enter the Earth's atmosphere.
Aquarium	Open—food for the organisms enters and waste is removed. Could be considered closed if time frame is limited.
Biosphere II in Arizona	Closed—only energy leaves. However, it could be argued that it can be open (eg when the CO_2 levels were manipulated, or when humans enter and leave).

Further exploration

- Some students will not be aware of Biosphere II. Use this as an opportunity to undertake some research about Biosphere II and a more local example of a closed system or eco centre. Ask students to compare and contrast Biosphere II with other similar projects.
- Have students evaluate the utility of projects like Biosphere II. Ask them if they think this is an efficient use of resources and money or what the benefit/cost of such projects is.

WEB LINKS

Visit the "Learn with us" section of the Eden Project site: www.edenproject.com

For further information on closed systems visit: www.nasa.gov/pdf/176994main_plugin-176994main_HSE_TG2-1.pdf

TIP

The examples of the aquarium and Biosphere II as open or closed systems are debatable. Allow students to argue their case using evidence for their statements. This is an excellent opportunity to highlight the need for specific definitions in science so that evidence can be evaluated appropriately. If definitions are not specific or detailed enough evidence becomes less conclusive.

Activity 2 Using Kepler's laws

In this activity, students are required to create structure and order from observations. This highlights the use of mathematics in science and how models of systems are useful for understanding connections between the components of a system.

Students will need to rearrange the equation in order to calculate the missing quantities and they will need a scientific calculator.

For the semi-major axis:

$$a = \left(\frac{T^2}{3 \times 10^{-4}}\right)^{\frac{1}{3}}$$

$$T = \sqrt{3 \times 10^{-4} a^3}$$

> **TIP**
>
> If students are out of practice regarding rearranging equations, provide a couple of easy equations to help prepare them, or solve the equation for a as a class before the students solve T individually.

Planet	Semi-major axis (10^{10} m)	Period T (years)
Mercury	5.79	0.241
Venus	10.8	0.615
Earth	15.0	1
Mars	22.8	1.886
Jupiter	77.86	11.9
Saturn	143	29.62
Uranus	286.51	84

For the second question, students will need to apply the principles they have studied about planets orbiting the Sun to satellites orbiting the Earth. They also need to consider how fast the Earth is rotating and, therefore, how fast the satellite needs to move.

Students should first consider the orbital path of the satellite. Polar orbiting satellites pass above (or nearly above) both poles, at right angles to the equator. Geostationary orbiting satellites move directly above the equator and, if moving at an appropriate, constant speed, their position remains constant for a stationary observer on Earth.

Students should identify that the period for the satellite orbiting the Earth needs to equal the time it takes for the Earth to rotate once. However, they cannot use the constant in the equation above because the longest diameter of orbit has changed because the orbit is now around the Earth, not the Sun.

It is possible to provide students with the new constant, but this is an excellent opportunity to stretch and challenge them. Using Kepler's third law in full:

$$\frac{T^2}{r^3} = \frac{4\pi^2}{GM}$$

students can find the radius of the orbit of the satellite from the Earth's core, knowing that T must be equal to one day. This is also an opportunity for students to research the constants G (universal gravitational constant) and M (mass of the body being orbited) and use these to calculate the required radius of orbit of the satellite for it to be geostationary.

$$G = 6.673 \times 10^{11} \text{ N (m/kg)}^2$$

$$M \text{ for Earth} = 5.972 \times 10^{24} \text{ kg}$$

> **TIP**
>
> Students can practise using a spreadsheet programme to calculate their missing values and compare these to their calculated values. Students often forget to include brackets, which will make their answers incorrect. This serves as a reminder that students should always verify their calculations.

> **DP LINKS**
>
> In physics, Topic 6.1, students will study Newton's law of universal gravitation; in Topic 9.4, they will derive Kepler's third law.

Further exploration

Students can be asked to calculate the speed at which the satellite will be moving using the equation

$$\frac{2\pi r}{T} = v$$

TEACHING IDEA 1

Some students might find it difficult to conceptualize the orbiting of a satellite around the Earth. Either create a model yourself, or ask the students to create one that demonstrates the movement of the Earth and a satellite. The process of creating a representative model can often help students visualize the entities they are studying and can highlight or refute misconceptions about the system being studied.

TIP

For a geostationary orbiting satellite, the distance to the centre of the Earth is 42,000 km with a speed of 31 km/s, assuming the orbital period of 23 hours and 56 minutes is used.

Activity 3 — Thermoregulation

This activity shows how the components of a system respond to change. Students are required to investigate how and why the body responds to changes in temperature using specific responses as examples.

Thermoregulation is a complex process, so this activity should be used conceptually to illustrate how systems respond to change. If appropriate, the concept of negative feedback could also be introduced, as it is so common in biological systems.

Students will need to understand the following principles about thermal energy transfer:

- Thermal energy can be transferred by conduction, convection and radiation.
- The blood can lose/gain thermal energy from other tissues and the air.
- Thermal energy can pass through body tissues.

Students also need to understand the principles of diffusion and gradients.

DP LINKS
In biology, students will study feedback systems in Topics 6.6 and 11.3.

Response	Temperature change	Mechanism
Shivering	colder	Shivering is muscles contracting and relaxing. This releases heat as a product of respiration.
Sweating	hotter	Water/sweat absorbs the heat from the body. Once enough thermal energy is absorbed, the water evaporates, taking the energy away and thus cooling down the person.
Goosebumps and erect body hair	colder	Hairs stand on end, thus trapping the air next to the skin. As the air next to the skin is warmer than the surrounding air, this traps the thermal energy closer to the body.
Reducing blood flow to extremities	colder	The further the blood travels away from the core, the colder it will become as it loses thermal energy to the surroundings. This response prevents loss of thermal energy from the blood.

TIP

Students find it easier to relate to a concept when it is directly related to their own lives. Ask students to run around and record the changes in the body that they can observe. If possible, move the students to a cooler place as well. If this is not possible, find some video clips to demonstrate these changes.

Ensure that locations are neither too hot nor too cold and in line with school safety procedures.

Students will need to think about gradients. The countercurrent flow works as there is always a heat gradient maintained, allowing heat to move from the arteries to the veins along all sections of the blood vessels. To help students understand, it is worth highlighting that at each section of the vein, the closest section of the artery is always warmer, thus heat will always travel from the artery to the vein.

TEACHING IDEA 2

The countercurrent flow can be modelled using two lines of students and some balls. The students represent blood and the balls represent heat. One line of students is the blood in the artery and the other is the blood in the vein. Students in the arteries start with 5 balls while those in the vein have none. The lines start at opposite ends of the classroom. As they pass each other, the students give a ball to another student if they have fewer balls. As arteries move further away from the core, they lose heat to the veins, enabling both vessels to retain heat.

Summary

Systems are common to all sciences. By understanding that all systems are a series of interacting components, students learn to connect ideas and to structure their knowledge. They can therefore create models to help clarify understanding of a component and its interaction within a given system as well as to enable further investigation of a particular idea.

Introducing key concept 2: change

	ATL skills	Science skills
Activity 1 Physical and chemical changes	✓ Listen actively to other perspectives and ideas.	✓ Make connections between relevant information to draw conclusions.
Activity 2 Human changes to global cycles	✓ Inquire in different contexts to gain a different perspective.	✓ Analyse information to draw justifiable conclusions.
Activity 3 Analysing possible causes for differences in electricity usage	✓ Practise visible thinking strategies and techniques.	✓ Interpret the relationship between two variables. ✓ Distinguish between correlation and cause and effect.
Activity 4 The precautionary principle	✓ Collect and analyse data to identify solutions and make informed decisions.	✓ Make connections between scientific research and related moral, ethical, social, economic, political or environmental factors.

Introducing change

Change is a shift from one state to another and can be viewed across systems over time. By investigating the process of change, students are able to understand how the world has been shaped in the past, the effects we see today, and the possibilities for change in the future. By understanding the causes and consequences of change, students will be able to make informed decisions regarding the future of the world.

Students are always interested to investigate the causes of particular events or processes, and the exploration of these can often lead to the synthesis of new knowledge and understanding. Students can then apply their knowledge to predict the consequences of change and use this to evaluate whether or not the impact will be beneficial.

In this chapter, students will learn to identify and suggest possible changes in a system and predict the consequences of them. Students will analyse data to draw conclusions about the causes and consequences of change, using mathematics as a tool to support their conclusions.

Activity 1 **Physical and chemical changes**

This activity requires students to identify the type of change that is occurring and then suggest whether it is reversible or not. Students tend to find that it is easier to identify the type of change than the reversibility of the change. The discussion aspect of this task is extremely important. Many students will have misconceptions about the underlying causes for the changes, and being able to discuss these in a group is important for clarifying understanding.

This activity also provides an excellent opportunity to debate ideas and concepts that are commonly accepted. It is commonly taught that all physical changes are reversible and all chemical changes are irreversible. However, there are many examples of chemical reactions that are reversible.

ammonium chloride $\rightleftharpoons$ ammonia + hydrogen chloride

anhydrous copper(II) sulfate + water $\rightleftharpoons$ hydrated copper(II) sulfate

Students might also approach these problems from a practical real-life situation. For example, when butter melts, this is a physical change. But the process of melting butter in a pan over heat is likely to cause a chemical change as well, as seen when the butter browns or burns.

Students may find it difficult to think about how it could be possible to reverse the breaking of glass. They might find it interesting to research how glass objects are made and, as a result, have a better understanding of the physical changes that can be made to glass.

Change	Physical or chemical?	Reversible or irreversible?
Popping popcorn	physical	reversible
Melting butter for popcorn	physical	reversible
Exploding fireworks	chemical	irreversible
Rusting an old bicycle	chemical	irreversible
Frying an egg	chemical	irreversible
Breaking glass	physical	reversible
Burning paper	chemical	irreversible
Freezing ice cubes	physical	reversible

TEACHING IDEA 1

Discuss all the changes as a large group to avoid continuation of misconceptions and enable students to share their ideas.

TEACHING IDEA 2

Demonstrate the examples of change in the lab. If possible, have the students conduct the changes themselves. Provide an ice bucket or equivalent and ask students to attempt to reverse some of the changes they have made.

TIP

Students often struggle with the difference between chemical and physical changes. Some observable features look like chemicals have changed (eg popping popcorn) but it is important to obtain as much data as possible before concluding. Provide extra information about the chemical composition of a kernel and popcorn to illustrate this point. This is also a debatable example. How can we be sure no chemical reaction has taken place? Can we be sure it is possible to reverse the reaction?

Activity 2 Human changes to global cycles

Students are required to select an example of change from a system they know and describe the changes that occur (such as change of state from water vapour to rain or semi-molten magma to solid rock, or chemical changes such as nitrogen fixation). They will then need to reflect on the impact that humans can have on the changes they have identified.

 DP LINKS

In biology, students will study global cycles in Topics 4.3 and 4.4.

Students may have difficulty describing the changes. Provide a key word list for each cycle so the students can communicate accurately. Students might also struggle to identify the underlying cause of the change unless they understand the cycle in depth. It is therefore important to check their understanding of the cycles before beginning this activity. If you have a unit that includes the study of cycles, then this activity can follow on from this. Alternatively, allow different groups to research each cycle before undertaking this activity.

The most likely activity of humans to be identified is the burning of fossil fuels. It is important that students understand there are two impacts from this: increase in the levels of CO_2 in the atmosphere, and depletion of resources. Deforestation is another particularly damaging and extreme impact of human activity on the environment. Deforestation increases CO_2 in the atmosphere *and* removes the trees that can remove CO_2 as well. Use this example to highlight how one activity can have more than one consequence. Although the carbon cycle is a cycle and all the components interact, some processes (eg fossilization) take significantly longer than others (eg combustion of fossil fuels). It is important that the students understand that time is an important factor when investigating change.

Further exploration

An interesting extension is to discuss the consequence of human activity on humans as a direct consequence of the change in the cycle. How this compares to the impact on other organisms is another important idea to consider.

Students can also use their knowledge of how human activities affect cycles to reflect on their own impact on the cycles. Do they think they should change their habits and actions as a result of investigating the possible consequences? If they did change, what effect would they have? How can humans best limit the effects of their actions on the environment?

TEACHING IDEA 3

Create flow diagrams of the cycles and cut them up so that the arrows, labels and pictures can be moved around. Have students organize the diagrams as a revision task. The students can then add or remove sections of the diagram to model the impact of humans and analyse the potential consequences of these changes.

TIP

Students can often only highlight direct consequences. Encourage them to use the word "therefore" after each sentence to help them understand there will be many secondary consequences as a result of a change.

 CHAPTER LINKS

This activity can be linked to the previous chapter about systems. The cycles can either be investigated in isolation or as a concurrent set of systems. Depending on the approach, the impacts discussed could be very different. This is also an excellent opportunity to evaluate the impact of human activity on each cycle and assess which cycle is impacted the most, and which will have the most significant consequences. See also Topic 2 in Chapter 10 on consequences.

Activity 3 Analysing possible causes for differences in electricity usage

This activity leads students through the steps undertaken by scientists when they are investigating causes and consequences. If the students read ahead, they will have all the answers without thinking for themselves. Consider not using the book the first time students approach this problem. Allow students to compare their conclusions with those in the book once the task is complete. Students can also compare their "I used to think …; now I think …" statements with each other.

Further exploration

Some students will struggle with having their opinions challenged by new data. It is imperative that students are encouraged to keep an open mind to all new evidence and to assess each piece on its merits.

TEACHING IDEA 4

When evaluating evidence and possible conclusions to draw from data, students need to appreciate that some pieces of evidence are more valuable than others. It may help to ask students to organize pieces of evidence into categories based on which side of the argument they support.

One way of doing this is to use a weighing scale analogy. Ask students to write out the evidence on pieces of paper and place each piece on the correct side. If a piece of evidence is particularly good, perhaps they could use it twice. Whichever way the scales tip is the argument that the evidence supports. You can help the students visualize this by using a real-life scale and attaching the evidence papers to weights.

TIP

Consider asking students to exchange their "I used to think …; now I think …" conclusions and discuss in pairs. Articulation of ideas can sometimes help students justify their arguments or see errors in their thinking.

Students often struggle with percentage change. It is worth explaining what a 49% increase actually means. For example, many students may not be able to equate a 100% increase with doubling. This can lead to misconceptions about the extent of the change occurring. Students often find it helps to relate to money as an example.

 Activity 4 The precautionary principle

This activity is excellent for developing research skills. It will require significant time and careful appreciation of the evidence. Students will need to understand how to identify if a source is trustworthy and valuable or not. A lot of popular conspiracy theories as well as personal anecdotes are repeated and used as evidence without verification. It is imperative that students are taught how to assess the value of evidence. Encourage students to assess the data objectively, as they will often respond to their preconceived fears rather than data or evidence.

Some of the science underlying these topics is quite complex and a significant understanding of the science is required. Help students focus on the question by assessing the evidence with respect to policy and action, rather than researching the science involved.

DP LINKS

The precautionary principle is taught in DP biology Topic 4.4 and is also a TOK link in the DP syllabus.

CHAPTER LINKS

In Chapter 6 on evidence, students will also learn how to evaluate the validity of data, looking at a variety of sources.

Summary

In this chapter, students have learned about the causes and consequences of change at both small and global scale. They should now understand the difference between chemical and physical change and that some changes are irreversible. Students should now be able to predict the effects of change, particularly in global cycles such as the carbon cycle.

They have also learned that it is necessary to bring time and care to the assessment of sources of information when seeking evidence, particularly when using the Internet and especially when researching contentious subjects involving change on a global scale.

CHAPTER 4

Introducing key concept 3: relationships

	ATL skills	Science skills
Activity 1 Prevention of malaria	✓ Collect and analyse data to identify solutions and make informed decisions.	✓ Analyse information to make a reasoned argument. ✓ Use appropriate scientific terminology to make the meaning of your findings clear.
Activity 2 Relationship between climate and sugar content in grapes	✓ Interpret data.	✓ Analyse information to make a reasoned argument. ✓ Process data and plot scatter graphs with a line of best fit to identify relationships between two variables.

Introducing relationships

Relationships are the connections and associations within and between entities. These entities can be objects, organisms, systems, forces, properties or even ideas. Through observation and experimentation, relationships between variables can be identified. Further experimentation can test these relationships so that theories can be established. By understanding the relationships of processes within the sciences, students can inform their own view of their position in the world.

This key concept enables students to link their knowledge and ideas from various topics. As students progress through the course, it is important that they are able to make connections within and between topics to understand how aspects interact and are related to each other. Learning about ideas in isolation prevents students from integrating material and thus limits their understanding. Every branch of science and all scientific ideas are part of many systems that interrelate. Investigating the relationships of these systems enables students to understand the interconnectivity of the sciences.

In this chapter, students will learn how to identify and communicate ideas about relationships, and how the consequences of actions can be predicted by investigating relationships. Students will use a variety of methods to identify and investigate relationships, reflecting on the scientific method as they proceed.

Activity 1 Prevention of malaria

Students are required to conduct research into the possible methods of malaria control. It is imperative that students research the underlying science of how the methods of prevention work as well as the financial and logistical implications of implementation.

Students will need to understand:

- the lifecycle of *Plasmodium* and the relationships between the parasite, the *Anopheles* mosquito and humans
- the conditions that enable and prevent the life cycle of *Plasmodium*.

Although not essential, it would benefit students to know about genetic modification of organisms, as these are involved in modern methods of malaria control.

For the research element of this task the main methods are as follows:

Prevention of mosquito breeding

- Introducing sterile males. Male mosquitoes are sterilized with radiation and then reintroduced to the wild thus reducing the chances of successful reproduction.
- Oil drip. A layer of oil on water prevents larvae from accessing the air with their breathing tube, and also prevents mosquitoes laying eggs in water.

Prevention of mosquitoes entering houses

- This involves traps or nets. There are many different varieties of net available but they all function in a similar way so be sure students do not spend too much time researching this.

Prevention of mosquito bites

- There are many varieties of insect repellent, and students should focus on the underlying science rather than the different brands.

Killing mosquitoes with insecticides

- DDT. Although there are many other insecticides, this is the most commonly used and widely referenced. Students will be able to find sufficient information to be able to fully evaluate the use of DDT.

Treating those infected

- Most treatment is based on antimalarial drugs (eg quinine), which kill the parasites.
- Testing for malaria normally involves examination of blood films. To help students understand the usefulness of these, it would be worthwhile to find sample pictures to show how malaria can be identified.
- Antigen tests are also possible, but in order to understand this method, students would need to know about antigens and the immune system.
- Keeping records of infection makes it possible to track the spread of malaria. Understanding how the disease spreads makes it possible to identify the best method of prevention. This increases the efficiency and efficacy of malaria control. This is a good demonstration of how data collection and trend identification can help solve local and global problems.

When students construct their recommendation it is important to ensure they use appropriate biological language. Many students will read generic sources that discuss non-science-specific ideas and it is important to maintain a scientific focus.

The term "most effective" is subjective, and students might look at relative cost to number of lives saved or perhaps at ease of completion. They can also link to cultural or religious beliefs about the treatment of animals and the role humans play in an ecosystem. It is easy for students to conform to their own cultural norms and this is an excellent opportunity to invite them to consider the beliefs of others.

DP LINKS

In biology, there is no explicit study of malaria in the core material. However, there are links to Topics 8.1 on metabolism (brief discussion about using databases to find new antimalarial drugs) and 3.1 on genes (brief discussion about link between sickle cell anaemia and malaria), and a link to option C.3.

TIP

Provide some initial stimulus material before the students conduct their own research. This will help students focus on the key ideas, and thus increase the efficiency of their research.

INTERDISCIPLINARY LINKS

Individuals and societies

The use of DDT is now banned in most developed countries as a result of the multitude of negative effects on the environment and human health. Students could research the history and use of DDT reflecting on the cost/benefit of using DDT in developing countries.

Students are often told that it is important to care about what happens in other countries, but have never considered why. The final question is excellent for stimulating debate to encourage students to share their ideas and use evidence to support their arguments.

Further exploration

1. Many solutions presented have other, negative consequences. Many of these were unforeseen when the interventions were initiated, but are worth discussing in order to prevent similar issues in the future. These include:
   - drug resistance of mosquitoes
   - hazards associated with taking blood tests, especially given the high incidence of HIV in regions with malaria
   - impact on ecosystem and other organisms with fewer mosquitoes
   - developing countries relying on developed countries for advanced technologies.

2. There is also the possibility of discussing other forms of biological control such as using natural predators. Obviously, this comes with associated positive and negative consequences. Ask students to reflect on how this relates to the precautionary principle discussed in Chapter 3 on change. Discuss if some methods violate this principle.

3. Because mosquitoes transport *Plasmodium*, it is commonly claimed that mosquitoes are the deadliest animal in the world, killing more people than any other. Compare the number of deaths from malaria to those caused by other animals and discuss potential reasons why we might fear other animals more. This is an excellent opportunity to relate ways of knowing (perception, emotion, logic) to our opinion of the world.

4. Students usually find the arguments for malaria prevention easy to understand. The idea of saving many human lives by killing another animal seems logical and reasonable. However, this is an excellent opportunity to challenge students to think critically. Ask the students if they think it is right to kill the mosquitoes. They are animals, after all, so ask students to imagine if the carrier organism that infected humans were a cat or dog, or even another human.
   - Would it be acceptable to kill the carrier in this situation?
   - Compare the case of mosquitoes carrying *Plasmodium* to humans carrying HIV.
   - Discuss the similarities and differences of prevention methods.

TIP

Allow students to prepare their recommendation in any medium. Some ideas are easier to represent in non-written media. This will facilitate the presentation of all ideas to the entire class without being repetitive. It will also help students develop IT literacy and communication skills.

👤 Activity 2 — Relationship between climate and sugar content in grapes

This activity is excellent for teaching how to analyse graphs and data and draw conclusions about relationships from this analysis. Students will need to be able to calculate percentage change to complete this task.

Students might have different views on the consumption of alcohol and there will be different legal and moral regulations influencing students, resulting in interesting but potentially difficult discussions.

The term "large increase" is very subjective and allows students the chance to discuss what constitutes "large". The absolute increase is very small in this example, but it is important for students to understand that relative change can often be a better reflection of the extent of a change than an absolute value. Ask the students to calculate the percentage increase from 1980 to 2008 (~10%), and also from the starting point of their trend line to the end point. For high-achieving students, this is an excellent opportunity to discuss the use of mathematics and statistics to provide an objective measure of change.

In step 5, most students will focus on the increase in temperature. Challenge the students to uncover other potential consequences such as increased levels of CO_2, changes of climate in different regions, transport costs, etc. For this, students will need to understand the global cycles as discussed in Activity 2, Chapter 3 on change.

🔗 DP LINKS
In biology, students will study photosynthesis in Topics 2.9 and 8.3.

Answers

In step 1, from the gradient of the graph, students should find that the increase is about 0.09 °Bx/year. In step 3, the potential alcohol content from grapes grown in 1980 is about 13.2%, and for grapes grown in 2008 is about 14.0%. In step 5, possible suggestions for how wine-makers may deal with this problem in the future could include the blending of different grape varieties, harvesting the grapes at different times and growing the grapes in artificial conditions.

TIP

Use this activity to highlight the subjective nature of lines of best fit and why they are appropriate in some circumstances but not others. This can be done by asking students to compare their lines with each other. This is also an opportunity to discuss the use of straight and curved lines and why each could be used in this situation. The trend does seem to be accelerating so a smooth curve might give a better fit (the gradient has been steeper in recent years).

Summary

In this chapter, students will have come to appreciate that making a change in a system to achieve a desirable goal requires considerable understanding of the components of that system and their relationships. For example, to formulate possible control methods for malaria requires understanding of the lifecycle of the *Plasmodium* parasite and its relationships with its hosts the *Anopheles* mosquito and humans. It also requires understanding of the relationships between the mosquito's breeding and feeding habits and humans.

Activity 2 demonstrates a relationship between climate and sugar content in grapes and also raises a different sort of relationship—that of relativity. Students learn that a tiny absolute change can also be a relatively large change. At the same time, they come to understand that small and large are subjective terms and it is important to use statistics to provide objective measures.

Energy

	ATL skills	Science skills
TOPIC 1 Energy content of diets		
Activity 1 Measuring the energy content of different foods	✓ Evaluate evidence and arguments.	✓ Organize and present data in tables ready for processing. ✓ Interpret data gained from scientific investigations and explain the results using scientific reasoning.
Activity 2 Monitoring dietary energy intake	✓ Collect and analyse data to identify solutions and make informed decisions.	✓ Organize and present data in tables ready for processing.
Activity 3 Analysing dietary energy from saturated fat	✓ Organize and depict information logically.	✓ Plot scatter graphs and identify trends.
TOPIC 2 Energy changes in chemistry		
Activity 4 Endothermic and exothermic changes	✓ Draw reasonable conclusions and generalizations.	✓ Organize and present data in tables ready for processing. ✓ Interpret data gained from scientific investigations and explain the results using scientific reasoning.
Activity 5 Energy transfer between hot and cold water	✓ Use and interpret a range of discipline-specific terms and symbols.	✓ Organize and present data in tables ready for processing.
Activity 6 Investigating a factor affecting the final temperature of a reaction mixture	✓ Test generalizations and conclusions.	✓ Design a method for testing a hypothesis, and select appropriate materials and equipment. ✓ Explain how to manipulate variables, and how enough data will be collected. ✓ Describe improvements to a method, to reduce sources of error, and possible extensions to the method for further inquiry.

Activity 7 What plant source is the best source of oil for biofuels?	✓ Collect and analyse data to identify solutions and make informed decisions.	✓ Formulate a testable hypothesis. ✓ Design a method for testing a hypothesis, and select appropriate materials and equipment. ✓ Explain how to manipulate variables, and how enough data will be collected. ✓ Organize and present data in tables ready for processing.
Activity 8 Investigating a model wind turbine	✓ Interpret data.	✓ Formulate a testable hypothesis. ✓ Design a method for testing a hypothesis, and select appropriate materials and equipment. ✓ Explain how to manipulate variables, and how enough data will be collected. ✓ Organize and present data in tables ready for processing. ✓ Interpret data gained from scientific investigations and explain the results using scientific reasoning. ✓ Evaluate the validity of the method. ✓ Describe improvements to a method, to reduce sources of error, and possible extensions to the method for further inquiry.
Activity 9 Marshmallow fusion	✓ Use models and simulations to explore complex systems and issues.	✓ Evaluate the validity of a model based on the outcome of an investigation.

Introducing energy

In this chapter, students will study the concept of energy by investigating diets and nutrition, energy changes in chemistry and the sustainability of energy resources. There is a strong focus on quantitatively measuring energy changes in different forms. This enhances the practical application of mathematics within the sciences.

Energy is an ideal concept to highlight relationships between the three sciences. It also provides an excellent context for studying the key concepts. We systematically classify energy into different forms and the transfer of energy is crucial to the function of systems. An understanding of the way in which energy is able to change form helps students understand complex processes and the relationships between various components of a system.

TOPIC 1 — Energy content of diets

In this topic students focus on energy in diets. The activity evaluating health claims about forms of energy in diets links well to Chapter 6 on evidence. Students also compare experimental values of energy content in a sample of food to the literature value. The activity on the energy content of food links to Chapter 7 on transformation.

This topic will promote some of the skills of scientific investigations including organizing and analysing data.

🔗 CHAPTER LINKS

See Topic 3 in Chapter 11 on form for a reminder of the forms of energy, and Topic 2 in Chapter 7 on transformation for a discussion of transformation of energy.

 Activity 1 — Measuring the energy content of different foods

[SAFETY]

This activity investigates how different types of food preparation or cooking affect the energy content of food and therefore involves students working with foodstuffs and boiling water.

Ensure students take due care when handling hot water, wear eye protection and tie back long hair. Students should not eat any of the food materials while in the laboratory. No student with an allergy to nuts should handle them or burn them. A student with a severe peanut allergy cannot be in the laboratory where peanuts are being burned.

Students should create a data table in advance. Encourage students to peer assess each other's tables before beginning. Data tables should contain the following fields:

- Mass of food (g)
- Mass of remaining material (g)
- Difference (g)
- Mass of water (g)
- Temperature of water before (°C or K depending on previous teaching)
- Temperature of water after (°C)
- Difference (°C)
- Heat produced by entire sample (calculation) (J)
- Heat produced per gram (J/g)
- Reference value (J/g); may involve a conversion depending on the source.

TIP

This experiment provides an opportunity for teachers to provide or review instruction on safety protocols related to fire. Remind students what to do in case of a burn. You might also discuss the different categories of fire extinguisher and the types of fire they are designed for. Ask students to predict the best type of fire extinguisher for the types of fire that might result from this practical activity.

This activity is useful as it reinforces a number of simple laboratory techniques, and how to collect, organize, transform and present data. You can use this as an opportunity to reinforce the idea of precision in data collection and how to estimate the last recorded digit to the nearest half of the smallest division on the scale of an analogue instrument. For example, to the nearest 0.5 °C if the smallest scale division on a thermometer is 1 °C. The requirements of "sufficient" relevant data can also be discussed in the context of this experiment.

Some foods are more flammable than others. Crisps (potato chips), roasted nuts and cheese curls are good choices as they are high in oil or fat and so ignite more easily.

Students will need to note that not all of the thermal energy from the flame is transferred to a temperature rise in the water (discussed further in Activity 2). Values are more likely to be related to the energy content due to fat.

Further exploration

Encourage students to compare the energy content of different forms of the same food (eg in a sample of mixed nuts). A challenge question is whether it is the surface area of the nut, the mass of the nut or the type of nut which matters more in the energy release.

Give the students some examples of calorie measurements and ask them to convert the data to joules. This can help them make decisions about what things have to be measured when designing the data table.

> **⊂⊃ DP LINKS**
>
> Within the DP science curriculum, there is a focus on the *Nature of Science* and *Theory of Knowledge*. Several knowledge questions arise in this topic.
>
> - How do scientists make decisions about which measurement standard to follow?
> - Why is the metric system preferable to others?
> - What are the causes and consequences of standards such as the often-cited dietary energy intake recommendation of 2,000 kilocalories per day for a woman?
>
> In DP biology, students studying option D explore a number of dimensions of human nutrition.

 Activity 2   Monitoring dietary energy intake

Do not insist that students share information about their weight or other results; they should be free to volunteer. This might lead to a class-based discussion about informed consent and choice as experiment subjects.

Encourage the students to discuss barriers to healthy eating such as pressure to maintain appearance, limited access to healthy alternatives, cost factors, time pressure, etc.

Students have difficulty remembering to track all of what they consume. If students work in teams they might be able to encourage each other to remember. Introducing frequent interim "homework" checks during the time period of the study might ensure broader compliance with the tracking process.

Further exploration

- Students can extend their investigation to include other nutrients such as dietary fibre. This would be a useful link to a discussion about the relationship between dietary fibre and colon health.
- Encourage students to evaluate their diet in terms of improving balance and healthy choices.
- Assign students a particular profile such as a teenager, pregnant woman, athlete, elderly person and ask them to conduct research about the unique dietary needs of a person with that profile.
- Particular nutrients have associated health risks (eg sodium and fructose). Ask students to track consumption of these elements in their diet.

> **⊂⊃ DP LINKS**
>
> Within the DP biology syllabus, students are asked to compare the suitability of lipids and carbohydrates for long-term energy storage in humans. Students are also asked to note that malnutrition may be caused by a deficiency, imbalance or excess of nutrients in the diet.

> **⊂⊃ WEB LINKS**
>
> The Food-A-Pedia feature on the website below allows students to conduct research on over 8,000 different foods:
> www.supertracker.usda.gov

Analysing dietary energy from saturated fat

In this activity students will construct a graph to visually compare the data from a number of European regions as well as the USA.

Provide students with a checklist of items for their graph, such as:

- a descriptive title that enables the chart to "stand on its own"
- label axes with the correct unit name and quantity
- plot the independent variable (the one that is varied, in this case % calories as saturated fat) on the *x*-axis
- plot all three sets of data on one graph
- a linear trendline is used
- indicate different series of lines with a descriptive key, not just "series 1".

DP LINKS

In DP biology, students evaluate the evidence for the health risk of saturated fatty acids.

In DP sciences, students are required to employ one of five types of ICT in their practical scheme of work. One of those five categories is the construction of a computer-generated graph.

INTERDISCIPLINARY LINKS

Depending on the level of statistics covered in the school's MYP mathematics programme, an R^2 value (the correlation coefficient) can be added to the trend line and students can discuss how well a straight-line model fits the data.

WEB LINKS

Video tutorials on how to use various software programs can be located on the Internet. For example, the search phrase: "How to create a graph using Google Docs" yields a number of training videos.

TOPIC 2 Energy changes in chemistry

In this topic, students will focus on the related concept of energy by studying thermochemistry. Thermochemistry deals with energy changes that accompany chemical reactions or physical changes such as phase change and dissolving. Specifically, students will investigate the difference between exothermic and endothermic changes by carrying out a series of reactions and monitoring temperature change. They will monitor how the amount of energy transfer is dependent on the volume/mass of a substance and the substance's specific heat capacity. They will design an experiment to investigate factors affecting temperature change in a reaction.

Before students start to investigate energy changes, you should ensure they understand the difference between physical change and chemical change. They must be able to use temperature collecting probes or thermometers. They also need to be familiar with elements of design—variables, data collection, hypothesis, method selection.

This is an effective introductory activity because students are provided with a series of energy changes that are either exothermic or endothermic. By monitoring the temperature change for each energy change, it is possible to classify the energy change as either exothermic or endothermic. The exact temperature change will depend on the exact amount of each reactant and factors such as the size of the mouth of the test tube. This is a great opportunity to discuss possible sources of error. You can continue this discussion throughout this chapter in relation to other calorimetry experiments. Some possible sources of error include: the amount of heat lost to the surroundings, not stirring evenly, missing the maximum temperature, error in the temperature recording device.

Instruct students to add a small amount of each solid (about the size of a peanut). You can easily substitute different substances, for example any metal or metal salt plus dilute acid. This activity is not about getting the "right" temperature change but about concluding which energy changes are exothermic and which are endothermic.

[SAFETY]
Note that 2M hydrochloric acid is an irritant. Ensure that eye protection is worn. Students must take due care to avoid contact with eyes, mouth and skin and wash off any chemical splashes on their skin with cold running water. Copper(II) sulfate solution is also harmful if swallowed and irritates the eyes and skin. Remind students to avoid skin contact with the copper(II) sulfate solution and to wash their hands immediately in the event of skin contact.

The student's data table should look like this:

Liquid	Solid	Initial temperature	Final temperature	Exothermic or endothermic
water	sodium nitrate			endothermic
water	ammonium chloride			endothermic
water	barium chloride octahydrate			endothermic
water	calcium chloride			endothermic
copper(II) sulfate	zinc metal			exothermic
hydrochloric acid	sodium hydroxide			exothermic
hydrochloric acid	calcium carbonate			exothermic
hydrochloric acid	magnesium			exothermic

 DP LINKS

This activity links with Topics 5 and 15 in the DP chemistry guide. Specifically, students will be required to perform calorimetry experiments regarding enthalpy changes and the associated calculations. They should understand the role that enthalpy of solution plays in an energy cycle.

Students need to understand the law of conservation of energy before doing the next activity, and be familiar with the idea of specific heat capacity and energy transfer calculations.

TIP

In the biology activities in this chapter, students use calorimetry techniques to calculate energy transfers. If Activities 1 and 2 have not yet been done, spend some time practising the calculations with students.

 Activity 5 | ## Energy transfer between hot and cold water

Students observe, by monitoring a change in temperature, how energy transfers occur when liquids at two different temperatures are mixed. The calculations should show that the energy lost by the warmer liquid equals the energy gained by the colder liquid (conservation of energy). Students should be able to conclude that the amount of heat that is transferred is dependent on the volume/mass of a substance and the substance's specific heat capacity. It is important to use an insulated container so that heat loss to the surroundings is minimized and the temperature change measured is representative of the energy transfer when the two solutions are mixed.

Further exploration

- Ask students to consider possible sources of error related to this procedure, and comment on how these errors could have affected their results.
- Ask students to hypothesize which procedure (A, B or C) would result in the greatest temperature change.
- Ask students to research geothermal heat exchange systems.

[SAFETY]

Ensure students take due care when handling hot water from the hot water tap, kettle, hotplate, Bunsen burner or spirit burner.

DP LINKS

This activity links with Topics 5 and 15 in the DP chemistry guide. Specifically students are required to perform calorimetry experiments regarding enthalpy changes and the associated calculations.

TEACHING IDEA 1

To extend the idea of energy change in chemistry, ask students to design their own thermometer or way of measuring temperature change. For this investigation, divide students into groups so that they can compete with each other to see who can design a thermometer that can provide the most accurate way of monitoring the temperature change in a chemistry reaction.

TEACHING IDEA 2

A possible extension to this activity could be to investigate the most efficient means of heating 50 cm^3 of water from room temperature to boiling. This will allow students to further investigate the idea of energy, but will also allow them to research different methods of providing heat and to design an experiment around this idea.

 Activity 6 | ## Investigating a factor affecting the final temperature of a reaction mixture

In this activity students will design and carry out an experiment to look at how the mass of baking soda used in a reaction with vinegar affects the final temperature of the reaction mixture.

Care should be taken with this reaction because there will be some mess to clear up. You may want to cover the work area with old newspaper or paper towels.

A quick demonstration is useful so students can see how violent the reaction is. This will allow them to create a detailed method and perform a trial test.

TOPIC 3 Sustainable energy resources

 TAKE ACTION
Students can raise awareness within the school community about different types of renewable energy and how these can be used to reduce global warming.

In this topic, students will focus on the sustainability of energy policies. They are expected to know about renewable energy sources. The activities and investigation in this topic are centred on increasing students' awareness of sustainable energy resources, including fusion power. They will discover why this is currently an inefficient way to generate power. Students will be asked to think critically about energy use and future energy supply, looking at both Africa and the EU.

Activity 7 What plant source is the best source of oil for biofuels?

Stage 1 of the unit planner

Key concept	Related concepts	Global context
Relationships	Energy Function Transformation	Globalization and sustainability
Statement of inquiry		
The current unbalanced relationship between global energy usage and available energy resources means that we have to examine ways of transforming non-traditional materials to alternative fuels.		

In this activity, students will investigate different plant sources of biofuel. Ensure students realize that they should use a consistent mass of plant sample during their testing (eg 2.0 g, 5.0 g). The mass is dependent on the size of the mortars and pestles and centrifuge that you have available. If you do not have a centrifuge, students can mix their ground plant source with water and leave to settle for a few days. The oil which rises to the top can be removed with a pipette.

CHAPTER LINKS
In Topic 1 Activity 1, students compare the energy contents of different foods by calculating the energy transferred per gram. In this activity students extend this calorimetric method to compare the energy output per 100 cm^3 of different oils.

DP LINKS
This activity links with option C in DP chemistry in which students investigate the chemical reactions involved in the formation of biofuels and evaluate the advantages and disadvantages of the use of biofuels.

Assessment

If you choose to assess students on this task, you can use criterion B. The task-specific descriptor in the top band (7–8) should read that students are able to:

- explain how evidence will be collected and manipulated to conclude the best primary source of plant oil for a biofuel
- formulate and explain a testable hypothesis—if plant source X is used then it will produce the greatest amount of biofuel
- explain how to manipulate the variables related to the extraction of biofuel from a plant source
- design a logical, complete and safe method in which they select appropriate materials and equipment in order to collect the greatest amount of biofuel from a plant source as possible.

Activity 8 Investigating a model wind turbine

Stage 1 of the unit planner

Key concept	Related concept(s)	Global context
Change	Energy Transformation	Globalization and sustainability
Statement of inquiry		
Modelling the transformation of energy from one form to another in order to demonstrate sustainability.		

Before this activity starts, students should know what the different forms of energy are. They should also know that a wind turbine can transform the kinetic energy of wind to kinetic energy of the rotor blades, which turn a generator to generate electricity. Demonstrate how a dynamo torch, like a wind turbine, can generate electricity, and how the bulb becomes brighter as you turn the handle faster. They should be aware that the voltage output of a generator (measured with a voltmeter) is a measure of the energy output. This investigation develops students' skills in designing an investigation and in evaluating results. It also reinforces what renewable energy is and how it works in the real world.

A good way to introduce this investigation could be through a discussion of renewable energy sources in the local region. Discuss which renewable energy source would be useful if you lived on a mountain. In this activity, students will change one aspect of the wind turbine. Most of the students will change the number, length or width of the blades. These changes will all increase the total surface area. The students should measure the voltage or power output so that they can graph their results. They may decide to link the windmill to a dynamo and measure the voltage output, or use string around a spindle to lift a small load and then calculate the work done in a measured period of time.

[SAFETY]

Fans should be clamped to stands that are G-clamped to the bench to prevent toppling.

Further exploration

Ask students to discuss and research how the power, once created by the wind turbine, is then moved efficiently to where it is needed.

Assessment

If you choose to assess students on this task, you can use criteria B or C.
The task-specific descriptor in the top band (7–8) should read that students are able to:

Criterion B

- explain the question about the wind turbine in detail and how they will test it with a scientific investigation
- formulate a testable hypothesis and explain it using correct scientific reasoning
- explain what variables they are using and how they are related to the hypothesis, explain how to manipulate and control the variables and how sufficient data will be collected by selecting at least five values of the independent variable and checking reproducibility of results
- design a logical, complete and safe method in which they select appropriate materials and equipment, including how each variable will be measured and (if appropriate to the method) how the data will be processed

Criterion C

- organize results in a suitable table, process data (calculating mean of repeat readings) and correctly present processed data as a scatter graph to aid understanding of the results
- accurately interpret data, identifying a trend from the graph, and explain results using correct scientific reasoning
- evaluate the validity of their hypothesis based on the outcome of their investigation
- evaluate the validity of the method, for example variables that were difficult to control
- explain how they could improve on this method to reduce sources of error and give more accurate results
- explain an extension to the investigation, using their results to develop a new line of inquiry (such as changing the independent variable to test its effect on the power output, or to investigate anomalies or unexpected results).

> ## QUICK THINK
> Students should be encouraged to do research on different designs used for wind turbines.

Activity 9   **Marshmallow fusion**

This activity demonstrates fusion in a very visual and hands-on manner. The students will observe that when the marshmallows are cool, they do not fuse together. When they are heated (as happens for fusion reactions in the Sun), the marshmallows fuse.

The students weigh the marshmallows so as to see the mass loss after heating (due to release of carbon dioxide during a combustion reaction). This analogy can be used to demonstrate the mass lost in fusion reactions, which the students can relate to the equation $E = mc^2$ as described in the chapter introduction, where there is also an example calculation for a deuterium–tritium fusion reaction.

TEACHING IDEA 3

An excellent video on fusion can be found on the EUROfusion website (www.euro-fusion.org) in the multimedia gallery.

Ask students to follow up the video by researching how much is being invested in fusion, and to explain why scientists believe this expenditure is justified. In their answers, they could refer to fusion versus fission as an energy resource, and also discuss fusion as a sustainable energy resource.

 DP LINKS

This topic links to the DP physics core Topics 7.2 and 8.1.

TIP

Students may confuse fusion and fission. Remember fusion means fusing nuclei together.

QUICK THINK

The EU quick think could be extended by getting the students to research whether all of the countries in the EU agreed to the proposals. Have an in-class discussion on the answers that the students put forward. They could also discuss different countries and how each country's policies have affected greenhouse gas emissions.

The flow chart is an excellent way to help the students discover how a growing population and a changing economy can change the face of how humans as a group over time can affect the environment around them.

Summary

The theme of energy is common to all sciences and is a fundamental component of scientific processes. As students further their understanding of how energy is transformed, they will be able to understand the implications for reactions in terms of energy and thus predict consequences of various processes.

The activities aim to provide opportunities to practise scientific and mathematical skills, and to demonstrate links between the sciences and the global importance of energy. Reflection on the implications of these links for individuals, groups and the world in general should offer the opportunity to students to place their knowledge about energy in context.

Evidence

	ATL skills	Science skills
TOPIC 1 Reasoning from evidence		
Activity 1 Testable statements	✓ Use brainstorming and visual diagrams to generate new ideas and inquiries.	✓ Formulate testable questions and hypotheses using scientific reasoning.
Activity 2 Developing hypotheses	✓ Make guesses, ask "what if" questions and generate testable hypotheses.	✓ Formulate testable questions and hypotheses using scientific reasoning.
Activity 3 Controlling variables in an investigation	✓ Give and receive meaningful feedback.	✓ Explain how to manipulate variables, and how enough data will be collected.
TOPIC 2 The role of evidence in chemistry		
Activity 4 Factors affecting reaction rates	✓ Process data and report results.	✓ Process data and plot scatter graphs with a line of best fit to identify relationships between variables. ✓ Interpret data and explain results using scientific reasoning.
Activity 5 Iodine clock reaction	✓ Process data and report results.	✓ Process data and plot scatter graphs with a line of best fit to identify relationships between variables.
Activity 6 Exploring the ethics of explosives	✓ Consider ideas from multiple perspectives.	✓ Make connections between scientific research and related ethical factors.
TOPIC 3 Big Bang theory—looking for evidence		
Activity 7 Visualizing the Doppler effect for sound	✓ Practise observing carefully in order to recognize problems.	✓ Formulate testable questions and hypotheses using scientific reasoning. ✓ Interpret data and explain results using scientific reasoning.
Activity 8 Hubble's evidence for redshift	✓ Apply skills and knowledge in unfamiliar situations.	✓ Process data and plot scatter graphs with a line of best fit to identify relationships between variables.

Introducing evidence

Science relies on evidence to support hypotheses, theories and laws. The scientific method requires us to search for evidence so that we can explain our observations. Throughout this chapter, students are required to evaluate hypotheses and conclusions in the light of the evidence they can gather. The activities in this chapter provide students with the opportunity to develop the skills required to obtain sufficient accurate and repeatable data from experimentation, enabling them to draw valid conclusions.

Students will learn how to evaluate the validity of data, both their own and other people's. By comparing and contrasting a variety of sources and searching for consistency of conclusions, students will also learn how to evaluate sources and thus develop their research and referencing skills. This concept is fundamental to their study, as students often cite their own or others' opinion as fact without any evidence to support these claims. While undertaking the activities, students will learn that conclusions about the natural world can only be based on evidence, and that scientific discussions only take place about conclusions that are based on the evidence, not on preconceptions or opinions.

DP LINKS

What constitutes evidence is a fundamental question addressed by the TOK curriculum. Students are often inclined to accept "facts" from a variety of sources without question. This chapter provides an excellent opportunity to discuss what is and is not acceptable as evidence in science. It also considers how to argue justification for something to be a valid piece of evidence.

TOPIC 1 — Reasoning from evidence

Evidence for knowledge claims in science comes from observation—often in the context of experiments. The activities in this topic are meant to focus on those aspects of criterion B related to setting a question, developing a hypothesis and devising a method to fairly test the hypothesis.

Activity 1 — Testable statements

This activity can be used to promote the skills of asking good questions, an expectation of aspect (i) of criterion B: *explain a problem or question to be tested by scientific investigation.*

This activity can be used to promote collaborative skills. Teachers can reinforce what constitutes good discussion behaviour (such as encouraging the ideas of others, actively contributing your own perspective and seeing the task through to completion). The ideal group size for many cooperative learning activities is four. It is often helpful to use a random group generator to select groups in an unbiased fashion.

Group work outcomes are improved if each individual is accountable for making a contribution. This can be enhanced by assigning roles such as *facilitator, recorder, interviewer, timekeeper,* etc. These roles can also be randomly assigned.

In step 2, students should complete a Venn diagram for each row of the table and compare the evidence required for each pair of statements in the same row. Once they have done this ask the students to develop a general list of the features of testable statements and the features of difficult-to-test statements.

WEB LINKS

A number of free web-based applications exist for generating random groups such as *Random Group Creator* at: www.aschool.us

Features of testable statements might include:

- they are focused
- they often contain both a dependent and an independent variable
- reading them immediately suggests a method you could develop to test whether or not they are true
- it is possible to be objective in testing them
- it is possible to establish criteria that can be used to judge whether the statement is true
- they can be used to make predictions
- it is possible to prove them wrong.

Features of difficult-to-test statements might include:

- they are vague
- it is difficult to establish criteria that can be used to judge whether or not the statement is true
- it is not clear what method could be followed to test the statements.

What they share in common:

- they can all be debated
- explanations for the statements can be provided, even if the statements are not true.

Example answers for Step 3

a) Plant biomass increases more for fertilized plants than unfertilized plants.

b) As concentration of salt in water approaches X, the percentage of brine shrimp eggs that hatch increases.

c) The number of trials required to condition a dog's behaviour is fewer than the number of trials required to condition a cat's behaviour.

d) The number of deaths during an earthquake is reduced by high-standard building codes.

e) Analysis of bones indicates that *Homo sapiens* had, in general, superior diet to *Homo neanderthalensis.*

f) This statement was included as an example of something that is, in fact, not testable. Discuss with your students why this is the case.

👤 Activity 2 — Developing hypotheses

This activity reinforces the "If … then … because …" framework for generating and justifying hypotheses. It can be used to reinforce aspect (ii) of criterion B: *formulate a testable hypothesis and explain it using scientific reasoning.*

Use this as an opportunity to clarify the distinction between dependent and independent variables.

Example hypotheses are included in the table below. Students should recognize that a number of alternate hypotheses are possible.

Question	If the (measured, or independent variable) is changed (in this way)	then the (dependent variable) will change (in this way)	because (use scientific reasoning to explain the hypothesis)
How does drinking coffee affect your heart rate?	**If the** amount of coffee consumed is increased	**then** heart rate will increase	**because** the caffeine found in coffee is a stimulant.
How does distance from the path affect the percentage of leaves that have been predated?	**If the** distance from the path is increased	**then** the percentage of leaves predated by herbivores will increase	**because** the density of leaves increases and the diversity of life (including more herbivores) increases with greater density of leaves.

Activity 3 Controlling variables in an investigation

In this activity students choose a hypothesis from the list in the student book and design and complete a safe method for testing it.

Designing an investigation as a group provides students with an opportunity to give and receive meaningful feedback as they work together.

Both experiments suggested in Activity 3 are relatively straightforward so students can design and carry out either. Both experiments illustrate the complexities of controlling for variables in systems (eg body systems, ecosystems).

The task can be used to assess criterion B formatively.

For activity (b), it would be helpful to carry out the experiment just after the grass is cut by school maintenance staff—at this time all areas will have a uniform height. Pinching grass blades off where they exit the ground and drying them for three days allows for comparison of above-ground dry biomass.

Further exploration

For activity (a), the biology and physics of scaling is a concept that could be explored in detail. Students could hypothesize and investigate which fitness tests favour people who have above-average height and which fitness tests favour people who have below-average height.

TOPIC 2 The role of evidence in chemistry

QUICK THINK

Students will examine videos of starting a campfire and food decomposing. Ask students to write down their observations. They can use this evidence to begin to think about how changing reaction conditions can affect the reactions that they will observe in the science lab.

Learning about the role of evidence in chemistry should enable students to interpret various forms of evidence (both primary collected data and evidence from secondary sources). Students should be able to determine whether or not the evidence is good enough to draw a valid conclusion. The focus in this topic is the study of kinetics (rates of reaction and factors that affect these rates). Students will investigate how evidence collected during experiments can be used to comment on how changing the reaction conditions can influence the rate of a reaction. Students will practise the skills of data collection, processing and graphical analysis. The details of the collision theory should enable students to explain why changing the reaction conditions can influence the rate of a reaction.

Students will also have the chance to explore the ethics of research into new explosives. Should such research be funded even though these chemicals would be capable of deadly consequences? What evidence would support continued research?

Before students investigate the role of evidence in experiments, you will want to ensure that they have practice in using basic apparatus for measuring volume and mass, and are able to measure with precision (to the smallest scale division) and accuracy (placing the eye at the same level as the meniscus of a liquid, zeroing the balance).

Activity 4　**Factors affecting reaction rates**

This introductory activity provides students with a specific reaction and detailed reaction conditions; they are told what data to collect and how frequently. After establishing baseline conditions in procedure A, students will investigate how changing various factors influences the overall rate of a reaction. By monitoring the change in total mass of reactants and glassware, students are measuring how changing the reactant conditions affects the rate of reaction.

Depending on class size, students can be divided into small groups (3 or 4 maximum) and each can be assigned a different procedure from which to collect data. Then they can pool their data in a class spreadsheet.

By examining the relative slope of each line and comparing it to the line produced by procedure A, students will be able to decide whether the factor changed in each procedure resulted in either a faster or slower rate than procedure A.

Students should conclude the following:

Rate is relatively slower when compared to procedure A	Rate is relatively faster when compared to procedure A
Procedure C	Procedure B
Procedure F	Procedure D
	Procedure E

[SAFETY]

2M hydrochloric acid is irritant. Ensure that eye protection is worn and that due care is taken when handling this chemical. Remind students to wash off any chemical splashes on their skin with cold running water.

Further exploration

If you want to extend the analysis for this activity, you can ask students to calculate the reaction rate for a certain period of time (between 30 seconds and 120 seconds). Calculating the slope of the line during that time will give students the reaction rate for that time period. They can then compare the rates quantitatively as well as qualitatively.

If you want to extend the data collection during this activity, you can provide some students with a syringe apparatus to collect data on the changing volume of carbon dioxide produced over time. Different groups can then compare their graphs. Encourage students to compare the two methods, and think about whether comparing the rate of loss of reactants produces the same conclusion as comparing the rate of gain of reactants. They could also evaluate the accuracy and precision of each method.

TIP

Ensure that students take a look at the complete data set before choosing the range for their graph. This will ensure that they can graph all six lines on the same graph.

DP LINKS

This activity links with Topic 6 in DP chemistry, where students will take a closer look at the rate of reaction. They will use kinetic theory to explain why changing factors (temperature, pressure/concentration and particle size) affects the rate of reaction. They will examine Maxwell–Boltzmann energy distribution curves, and will conduct and evaluate experiments to investigate reaction rates.

Activity 5 Iodine clock reaction

In this activity students will use their knowledge of reaction rates gained in Activity 4 to investigate how changing the concentration of a reactant affects the rate of reaction.

This reaction involves a series of intermediary steps and is therefore referred to as a complex reaction; it is not necessary for students to know the chemical equations for this reaction.

Students can collect both qualitative and quantitative evidence. There is a clear colour change that indicates that the reaction is complete. You may want to explain that the colour change occurs due to production of excess iodine, which turns dark blue in the presence of starch. Students should stop the stopwatch as soon as the colour changes. They will need to consider how much data is "sufficient" to form a valid conclusion.

It is important that students follow the same procedure (same pouring rate, same stirring rate, etc.) each time so that the conditions are consistent and will not affect the reaction time.

You will need to prepare fresh solutions of each of the following in sufficient quantity for all students to conduct at least five trials for each value of X drops of potassium iodate:

- 0.20M potassium iodate
- 1% soluble starch solution
- 0.20M sodium metabisulfite.

Students are asked to graph the data they collect. They first need to determine how best to manipulate their data—they should graph an average value of time for each value of X. This should produce a relatively straight line. Ask students for the significance of the straight line—the rate increases in proportion to the number of X, hence the rate changes in proportion to the concentration of potassium iodate. Students are asked to consider possible sources of error—these include human reaction time (the change happens instantaneously but different people react faster or slower). This is why the third decimal place in the time measurement (1/100th second) is uncertain and should be discounted. To reduce inaccuracies, students should take the mean of the class results for each concentration.

[SAFETY]

Concentrated sulfuric acid is very corrosive. Use the lowest possible concentration and do not place large bottles in the lab; use small, labelled dropper bottles that allow a single drop to be dispensed easily. Either yourself or a lab technician should provide the drop of acid to the students. Ensure that eye protection is worn and that due care is taken when handling this chemical. Remind students to wash off any chemical splashes on their skin with cold running water.

> **⊂⊃ DP LINKS**
> This activity links with Topic 6 in DP chemistry, where students will take a closer look at the rate of reaction, using kinetic theory to explain why changing factors (temperature, pressure/concentration and particle size) affect the rate of reaction and will conduct and evaluate experiments to investigate reaction rates.

 Activity 6 Exploring the ethics of explosives

By watching *PBS Nova: Kaboom!* students immerse themselves in the development of explosives across the centuries. As competition increases to produce the most powerful explosive in the most efficient manner, the pressure to research and develop new explosives increases. Students should be able to discuss that sometimes, even though the scientific knowledge and evidence from investigations indicate that the chemistry is possible, scientists have a moral obligation to consider the possible consequences of their discoveries in terms of harm to the environment and/or humans.

You may want to develop a debate centred on this topic and other ethical decisions that scientists have to grapple with.

> **⊂⊃ DP LINKS**
> This activity links with TOK and the ethics area of knowledge.

TOPIC 3 | Big Bang theory— looking for evidence

This topic is based on students developing an understanding of how we can use evidence to develop a theory—how evidence from the wavelength of light from distant galaxies helped develop the theory of the Big Bang. Students will discover certain properties of waves and what the light spectrum is.

Students first undertake an activity to demonstrate the properties of waves that led to the Doppler shift type of evidence that Hubble used. They will then analyse his data to discover the relationship for themselves. This will help students to think critically about evidence and theories developed from evidence. Throughout this topic, it is important to emphasize to students how evidence from one area of study can be used to develop theories in another area of study.

CHAPTER LINKS

This topic links well to Topic 3 in Chapter 8 on models, where students learn about different types of wave and their properties, and use a slinky spring to investigate wavelength, wave speed and interference.

Activity 7 | Visualizing the Doppler effect for sound

It is important that, before the activity, the students understand that sound and electromagnetic radiation (including light) move in the form of waves. They will therefore be able to relate what they observe to light waves as well as sound waves. They should also be aware of the terms "wavelength" and "frequency". Understanding the meaning of these terms is essential for understanding the Doppler effect.

Students will observe that sound from a source approaching you is observed as higher pitched than sound from a source receding from you. This is because the wavelengths of the waves from an approaching sound source become shorter. Their frequency is therefore increased, which is observed as a high-pitched sound. If the sound source is moving away from you, the wavelength of the sound waves is getting longer and the frequency will decrease, which will be observed as a low-pitched sound.

Further exploration

Ask students to discuss other situations in which the Doppler effect is observed in the real world.

Once the students have gained an understanding of the Doppler effect, they can relate this to the redshift observed from far-away galaxies and therefore discuss the theory of the Big Bang.

TIP

If students are struggling with their understanding of waves and the spectrum, refer to the text and diagrams on types of waves in Chapter 8 on models.

WEB LINKS

Search the BBC website for the Doppler effect. This site has excellent animations that translate to a whiteboard very well. It can help bring the Doppler effect to life for students.

Activity 8 | Hubble's evidence for redshift

It is important that the students understand the spectrum of light as explained in the student book, and the Doppler effect from the previous activity. A good way to introduce this activity is to discuss the light spectrum and how it can be linked to the Doppler effect.

The students must be able to create a scatter graph with a best fit line, by hand or using a spreadsheet.

DP LINKS

This topic links with DP physics Topics 4, 9 and 7.

Answer

Students should discover that there is a positive correlation between the distance a galaxy is from us and the velocity at which it is moving away from us.

Galaxies with the longest redshifted wavelength must be moving away from us the fastest. At this point the students should relate their graph to the Doppler effect. They have discovered that redshift is evidence for the expansion of the Universe—that all galaxies are moving away from the Earth, at speeds dependent on their distance from us.

Further exploration

Research where else in science a theory in one area has been used to effectively develop a theory in another area. For example, how electromagnetic waves (physics) have been used to improve medical research and our knowledge of the human body (biology).

Ask students to use their research skills to discover what CERN has proved to us. It is important that the students learn that CERN has given us a huge amount of data that is helping us discover more about the first moments after the Big Bang. The students could also look at the possibilities of CERN and LHC in the future.

TEACHING IDEA 1

Stronger students should be encouraged to research cosmic microwave background radiation, as this will test their understanding of waves and the Big Bang theory. They could do a presentation on this and link it to the rest of the material covered in this topic.

TEACHING IDEA 2

Students can use the following quotations as a starting point to look at scientists who were only proven right after their death.

QUOTATION

I am quite surprised that it happened during my lifetime. It is nice to be right about something sometimes.
Peter Higgs on CERN when scientists detected the Higgs boson particle

QUOTATION

*The LHC accelerates
the protons and the lead,
and the things that it discovers
will rock you in the head.*
Katherine McAlpine in her Large Hadron Collider Rap

 **WEB LINKS**
Go to:
www.home.web.cern.ch
where you will find teaching resources and lesson plans to help integrate CERN and the LHC into the classroom.

Summary

The evaluation of evidence is a crucial skill students will need in every aspect of their scientific studies. In this chapter, students have had the opportunity to generate evidence from which to draw conclusions. The skill of designing an experiment that produces sufficient accurate, repeatable and reproducible data is crucial for the sciences. Most notably, controlling variables is extremely important as it allows precise conclusions to be drawn about the interaction between dependent and independent variables. Students have had the opportunity to practise manipulating variables and should therefore be able to evaluate their own methods of data collection as well as data produced by others.

Transformation

	ATL skills	Science skills
TOPIC 1 Energy in food chains		
Activity 1 Investigating optimal conditions for the formation of plant biomass	✓ Gather and organize relevant information to formulate an argument.	✓ Design a method and select appropriate materials and equipment. ✓ Explain how to manipulate variables, and how enough data will be collected. ✓ Organize and present data in tables. ✓ Decide how the raw data should be transformed and presented into a form suitable for visual representation.
Activity 2 Comparing mealworms to traditional sources of protein	✓ Collect and analyse data to identify solutions and make informed decisions.	✓ Analyse data to draw justifiable conclusions.
Activity 3 Feed conversion ratios in mealworms	✓ Process data and report results.	✓ Design a method and select appropriate materials and equipment. ✓ Explain how to manipulate variables, and how enough data will be collected. ✓ Organize and present data in tables. ✓ Decide how the raw data should be transformed and presented into a form suitable for visual representation.
Activity 4 Interpreting your ecological footprint	✓ Collect and analyse data to identify solutions and make informed decisions.	✓ Draw conclusions, and explain these using scientific reasoning.
TOPIC 2 Transformation of energy and matter		
Activity 5 Beer foam decay curve	✓ Use models and simulations to explore complex systems and issues.	✓ Organize and present data in tables. ✓ Decide how the raw data should be transformed and presented into a form suitable for visual representation.

Introducing transformation

Transformation of energy and matter are continuous, occurring in many different manners in many different systems. Students will investigate the transformation of energy across the sciences and how the changing of energy between different forms explains natural phenomena. Students will also learn how we can manipulate transformations of energy and matter and apply this knowledge to solve problems and synthesize new ideas.

TOPIC 1 — Energy in food chains

This topic links well to Topic 1 in Chapter 5 on energy. Here, students explore energy transformations in food chains. The topics are related to the globalization and sustainability global context as students consider ethical food choices in relation to minimizing their ecological footprint. Integrated farming and alternate sources of protein are considered.

 Activity 1 Investigating optimal conditions for the formation of plant biomass

Stage 1 of the unit planner

Key concept	Related concept(s)	Global context
Relationships	Transformation Energy	Globalization and sustainability
Statement of inquiry		
Knowledge of the relationship between optimal conditions and the biological processes that transform light energy into chemical (biomass) energy can be used to maximize crop yields.		

[SAFETY]

If infrared or other heat lamps are used, it is important to avoid contact with water, and not to set them up or switch them on or off with wet hands. Good hygiene rules should be observed when handling duckweed. Ensure students wash their hands after doing so and keep skin contact to a minimum.

The activity is useful as it requires students to use their planning, research, perseverance and experimental skills.

Further exploration

Duckweed has become invasive in parts of the world. Students could conduct investigations into the various strategies organizations use to control the weed. Duckweed often grows in lakes that have low dissolved oxygen. Students can explore whether this is a causal relationship or simply a correlation. Dissolved oxygen levels can be raised with a bubbler or lowered by placing plant detritus at the base of the container.

TIP

Rather than measuring biomass directly, individual leaves or fronds can be counted and changes in this number can be used as a model of growth in biomass. Count all visible fronds, even the tips of small fronds that are only beginning to emerge. Counting can be time-consuming and might be expedited by using tools that allow for analysis of digital images.

The activity requires a lot of space as generation of sufficient relevant data requires a number of containers for each experiment. Therefore, it is better to carry out the experiment in groups.

WEB LINKS

The organization *Science and Plants for Schools* has a number of investigations related to growing duckweed, which can be found using the search term "Using Duckweed in the Lab":
www.saps.org.uk/secondary/teaching-resources/744-using-duckweed-in-the-lab

Assessment

If you choose to assess students on this task, you can use criteria B and C. The task-specific descriptor in the top band (7–8) should read that the student is able to:

Criterion B

- explain the reasons why growth in biomass is affected by both biotic and abiotic factors and the reasons why the question is significant
- formulate and explain a testable hypothesis regarding the impact that varying their chosen variable will have on biomass growth rates compared to controls using correct scientific reasoning
- explain the ways in which the experimental variable will be altered and how the other variables that could affect the plant growth will be controlled, and explain how sufficient plant growth data will be collected including the frequency of data collection and the number of replicate growth chambers that will be used
- design a logical, complete and safe method in which the student selects appropriate materials and equipment that takes into account available space and resources of the school laboratory.

> **TAKE ACTION**
>
> Invasive aquatic plants are a global problem. Encourage students to volunteer to support the removal of invasive species from local habitats.

Criterion C

- correctly collect and record biomass data and organize the data into a table, transform the raw data table using a suitable graph and present data for growth rates in numerical and visual forms
- accurately interpret data and explain the growth data using correct scientific reasoning
- evaluate the validity of the hypothesis regarding variables affecting biomass growth based on the outcome of the investigation
- evaluate the validity of the method based on the outcome of the investigation, identifying limitations and discussing their implications for the results
- explain improvements to the method and provide suggestions for further investigation that would benefit the investigation.

Activity 2 — Comparing mealworms to traditional sources of protein

This data-based question introduces the notion that land area is an input into food production.

Suggested answers

a) Approximately $20\ m^2$ (acceptable answers could range from $15-20\ m^2$).

b) While the data is variable, all estimates indicate that the amount of land required to raise beef is significantly more than for other forms of livestock production; the data only provides evidence of land inputs and not other inputs such as water or outputs such as waste.

In this activity students will design and carry out an investigation into one of the factors that lead to the maximum gain in biomass of mealworms over a three-week period.

Stage 1 of the unit planner

Key concept	Related concept(s)	Global context
Relationships	Transformation Energy	Globalization and sustainability
Statement of inquiry		
Knowledge of the relationship between feed inputs and edible protein outputs can be used to evaluate the sustainability of livestock production.		

This experiment provides an experience of the careful treatment of animals. Students should consult the IB animal experimentation policy in the biology teacher support material to ensure compliance with the principled behaviour outlined in this guide.

The concept of productivity can be learned through this experiment. Possible variables other than the types of food source given to the mealworms include: temperature (such as room temperature, close to a source of warmth and within the laboratory fridge), humidity (if a piece of fresh potato is included in the culture or not) or surface area of the culture. Ensure that the conditions are within the tolerance limits of the animals.

[SAFETY]

Ensure students wash their hands after handling mealworms. Students who suffer from allergies or asthma should take precautions when working with the worms.

Assessment

If you choose to assess students on this task, you can use criteria B and C. The task-specific descriptor in the top band (7–8) should read that students are able to:

Criterion B

- explain the reasons why the impact of their chosen variable on mass gain by mealworms is a question that needs to be addressed
- formulate a testable hypothesis and explain the reasons why mealworms gain mass differently than the control under the circumstances of their chosen variable using correct scientific reasoning
- explain how to manipulate the variables including how to control other variables that would impact the outcome, and explain how sufficient, relevant data will be collected
- design a logical, complete and safe method in which they select appropriate materials and equipment that also maintains conditions for the mealworms within tolerable limits.

Criterion C

- correctly collect and record mass data and organize the data into a table, transform the raw data using measures of central tendency and present the data in graphical form
- accurately interpret data and explain the mass change data using correct scientific reasoning
- evaluate the validity of their hypothesis regarding variables affecting mass growth based on the outcome of their investigation
- evaluate the validity of their method based on the outcome of their investigation, identifying limitations and discussing their implications for the results
- explain improvements to the method and provide suggestions for further investigation that would benefit the investigation.

DP LINKS

The concept of efficiency of energy transformation is further developed in DP physics in the mechanics unit. The concept of feed conversion ratios is further explored in option C of DP biology.

WEB LINKS

The website *Raising Mealworms: Everything You Always Wanted to Know* (and more) provides comprehensive information:
www.sialis.org/raisingmealworms.htm

A report from the UN entitled *Environmental Opportunities for Insect Rearing for Food and Feed* can be found at:
www.fao.org/docrep/018/i3253e/ i3253e05.pdf

TIP

Frass is the excrement of insect larvae and in the case of mealworms appears like sand. If oats or large bran flakes are used, it is possible to sift the frass away from the food. As the mealworms moult, they leave behind exoskeleton pieces. The number of moults before a mealworm becomes an adult varies between 6 and 20 and the length of time spent as larvae is about two months. The average mass of an individual is about 0.2–0.4 grams and changes in mass per day are between 0.01 and 0.04 so differences may be easier to detect in batches. Exoskeletons can be separated from feed but frass is more difficult to separate. If the container is left closed with air holes for gas exchange, loss of mass can be attributed to energy lost due to respiration.

This activity provides students with the opportunity to generate, interpret and explain data.

Further exploration

The concept of "food miles" can be investigated by students. It refers to the distance that food travels between its source and the location where it is consumed by its target market.

WEB LINKS

Search for "ecological footprint calculators". One such calculator allows you to do an analysis just by diet: www.foodday.org/14questions

TAKE ACTION

Encourage students to reflect on the sustainability and other ethical aspects of their food choices and perhaps change their food consumption patterns. They can consider: conditions of production for the animals, labour issues, distance the food travels to market, by-products of the production of the food, water consumption, land access issues in the country of production and a range of other issues.

TOPIC 2 — Transformation of energy and matter

The law of conservation of energy and the definition of "work done" are fundamental concepts of the MYP Sciences course. This topic provides a summary of energy transformation before exploring transformation of matter in radioactive decay.

Activities in this topic are centred on understanding what is meant by radioactive decay, and its characteristics and uses. Students will investigate how carbon dating is used to determine the age of the Earth. Activity 5 models radioactive decay. Students should be able to collect data and present their results on a graph that can be used to find properties of radioactive decay such as the half-life.

CHAPTER LINKS

The different forms of energy storage are described in Chapter 11 on form. Energy efficiency in relation to the law of conservation of energy is discussed in Chapter 5 on energy.

QUICK THINK

- Diesel vehicle: chemical energy stored in fuel → kinetic energy of moving vehicle
- Battery toy: chemical energy in the battery → kinetic energy of motor → kinetic energy of moving toy

In all cases, not all the energy stored in the fuel or energy store ends up doing useful work. Some energy is also transferred to the surroundings as heat and sound, and is stored in the surroundings as thermal energy.

QUICK THINK

Nuclear fission (eg of uranium-235) produces smaller nuclei (eg krypton-91 and barium-142), which may themselves be radioactive and undergo further decay, producing further radioactive isotopes (eg caesium-137 and strontium-90). Radioactive isotopes are also formed when materials in the reactor core absorb neutrons. Radioactive waste includes the radioactive starting material and the radioactive decay products. Some of these have very long half-lives and will remain radioactive for very long periods. This poses the problem of how to safely store this waste so it does not harm living things in the environment. Strontium-90: 28 years; caesium-137: 30 years; plutonium-239; 24,000 years; caesium-135: 2.3 million years; iodine-129: 15.7 million years.

The accidental release of radioactive isotopes is one of the problems associated with nuclear power.

TEACHING IDEA 1

Carbon dating can be used to provide evidence for evolution. To model this, ask the students to consider the case of Frosty the snowman. One day, Frosty began to melt. Ask the students to form groups and give them a measuring cylinder containing melting ice. This is the remains of poor Frosty. Ask them to work backwards to find out when Frosty the snowman began to melt.

Students will need to come up with a method to find out when Frosty started to melt. They should decide to record Frosty's melted remains (water) and note the time on the clock. Students should record the volume of water in the cylinder at regular intervals. Students should graph their data and use the graph to predict when Frosty began to melt.

Ask students to discuss how this investigation can be used to model carbon dating.

 Activity 5 Beer foam decay curve

In this activity students will look at the rate of decay of foam on beer as a model of nuclear decay.

Stage 1 of the unit planner

Key concept	Related concept(s)	Global context
Change	Energy Transformation	Globalization and sustainability
Statement of inquiry		
Transforming atoms through radioactive decay releases energy and may provide part of a sustainable energy resource strategy.		

[SAFETY]

The teacher should ensure there is no tasting or drinking of the beer or foam.

It is important to stress to students that this activity models nuclear decay. The purpose of the activity is to understand what is meant by the half-life of a particle and why the rate of decay of a particle decreases over time.

Students will model the rate of decay of particles (isotopes) by measuring the change in the height of beer foam over time. Before students start this activity they need to understand that radioactive decay is a random process (we cannot predict when it will happen) and, therefore, the time it takes for one particle (isotope) to decay cannot be measured accurately. A large sample of particles (isotopes) is taken to find the probability of a certain fraction of particles decaying in a certain time.

A good way to introduce this activity is to discuss with students what they think will happen to the frothy head of beer over time. Ask students to discuss why this is happening (ie what is happening to the individual foam bubbles—they are changing to liquid). Ask students if they think the number of beer foam bubbles popping will be greater, smaller or the same as time increases. The height of the foam is directly proportional to its volume, as the measuring cylinder is uniform.

In preparation for this activity, students should construct or be given a table to record their data. They should find that the slope of the graph decreases with time and that the half-life of the foamy head is reasonably constant. Different groups should obtain similar results showing that different starting volumes do not affect the half-life.

Once the students have completed the activity and answered the questions, they should accurately interpret how the data models radioactive decay and explain their results using correct scientific reasoning.

Assessment

If you choose to assess students on this task, you can use criterion C. The task-specific descriptor in the top band (7–8) should read that students are able to:

Criterion C

- correctly collect, organize, transform and present data for the change in height of beer foam in time in numerical form and correctly plot a scatter graph with line of best fit
- accurately interpret their data, identifying from the graph that the half-life is constant, and explain the results using correct scientific reasoning
- evaluate the validity of their hypothesis
- evaluate the validity of the method based on conditions of the experiment, fair testing procedure and whether enough data was collected to address the question

Further exploration

- Students can also research decay graphs of radioactive isotopes to show that the shape of their beer-foam decay curve is the same as that for radioactive isotopes. Students should then use the graphs they have found to find the half-life of different radioactive isotopes.

- Students can use their graph from the beer foam activity to determine the number of half-lives it took for the whole sample to decay. This activity can then be extended by finding the number of half-lives in a certain decay time for radioactive isotopes. Students should be able to see that although the half-life remains the same, the number of particles decaying decreases over time.

 **DP LINKS**

In DP physics, students are required to solve problems on radioactive decay involving only integral numbers of half-lives. In DP mathematics, students will investigate exponential and logarithmic functions in detail.

TEACHING IDEA 2

Here is another modelling activity that will help teachers explain the concept of half-life and the random nature of radioactive decay.

A set of dice can be used to model a sample of radioactive rock with each die representing a single radioactive atom. If, after a collective roll of all the dice, a die lands showing 6, this represents that it has decayed to a daughter nucleus, so it is removed from the sample.

Instructions:

1) To start, give each group a large number (10 or more) of six-sided dice. The group all roll their dice at the same time. Each roll represents the same time interval.

2) Any dice that land showing a 6 are counted and removed. The group makes a note of how many dice landed showing a 6 during that roll.

3) The remaining dice are rolled again, and again the ones that land showing a 6 are counted and removed. This is repeated until the group has run out of dice or has made ten rolls, whichever comes first.

4) Ask students to plot a graph of the number of remaining dice against the roll number and draw a smooth curve of best fit through the points. From this, ask them to calculate the half-life of their dice. For example, if they started with 10 dice, how many rolls did it take before there were 5 dice remaining? Students could also find the half-life from eight to four dice.

5) One group's set of results may not produce a smooth curve, due to the random nature of how many rolls it takes for half the dice to have produced a 6. However, repeat measurements of the same sample produce different counts. Collation of all results in the class will produce a graph that is less random.

6) To demonstrate that the size of sample does not affect the half-life, give different groups different numbers of dice.

Further exploration

- Ten-sided dice can be used to simulate the half-life of a different isotope. The graph should show a shallower slope as fewer atoms (dice) are removed in each trial.
- Provide a sample of equal numbers of six-sided and ten-sided dice to show that the numbers of each isotope (dice) remaining diverges over time.

◌◌ INTERDISCIPLINARY LINKS

In mathematics, students investigate functions and graphs of functions. Students could extend their knowledge of the radioactive decay curve and develop the function of this curve in mathematics.

TIP

Students can find it difficult to visualize radioactive decay. Getting students to make a comic strip or storyboard of how an isotope is transformed into another with the release of energy may help them remember the abstract topic.

Summary

In this chapter, students have learned how to apply their understanding of the transformation of energy and matter to unfamiliar situations. This will enable them to understand how scientific concepts can be explained in terms of transformation, and thus how each aspect of science is interrelated.

They have learned how to observe and manipulate transformations, integrating their knowledge across the sciences to solve problems and explain why certain processes occur. They have investigated transformation in the context of human interaction with the world. Students should be able to relate the impact of humans and subsequent transformations of energy and matter, as well as how humans can use their knowledge to help the development of novel ideas and further understanding of the world.

Models

	ATL skills	Science skills
TOPIC 1 Evaluating models in biology		
Activity 1 Modelling evolution by natural selection	✓ Use models and simulations to explore complex systems and issues.	✓ Evaluate the validity of a model based on the outcome of an investigation. ✓ Draw sketches of observations from an experiment.
Activity 2 Modelling movement across a cell membrane	✓ Use models and simulations to explore complex systems and issues.	✓ Evaluate the validity of a model based on the outcome of an investigation. ✓ Formulate a testable hypothesis using correct scientific reasoning.
Activity 3 Modelling osmosis in plant tissues	✓ Recognize unstated assumptions and bias.	✓ Evaluate the validity of a model based on the outcome of an investigation. ✓ Organize and present data in tables ready for processing.
Activity 4 Modelling osmosis in animal tissues	✓ Gather and organize relevant information to formulate an argument.	✓ Evaluate the validity of a model based on the outcome of an investigation. ✓ Organize and present data in tables ready for processing.
TOPIC 2 Models of atomic structure		
Activity 5 Bohr model of the atom and line spectra	✓ Make connections between various sources of information.	✓ Organize and present data in tables ready for processing. ✓ Draw sketches of observations from an experiment.
Activity 6 Mapping the inside of an atom	✓ Use and interpret a range of discipline-specific terms and symbols.	✓ Process and interpret data and explain results using scientific reasoning.
Activity 7 Isotopes— Beanium lab	✓ Use and interpret a range of discipline-specific terms and symbols.	✓ Process and interpret data and explain results using scientific reasoning.
TOPIC 3 Making waves		
Activity 8 Modelling transverse waves	✓ Draw reasonable conclusions and generalizations.	✓ Draw sketches of observations from an experiment.
Activity 9 Modelling wave interference	✓ Use models and simulations to explore complex systems and issues.	✓ Draw sketches of observations from an experiment.

Activity 10 Exploring wave speed	✓ Make guesses, ask "what if" questions and generate testable hypotheses.	✓ Design a method for testing a hypothesis, explaining how to manipulate the variables and how data will be collected.
		✓ Organize and present data in tables ready for processing.
		✓ Describe improvements to a method, to reduce sources of error.

Introducing models

Models can represent our observations and scientific concepts, and can also enhance our understanding by offering the opportunity to explore potential interactions and consequences in a variety of systems. Constructing their own models can help students further consolidate their understanding. By evaluating models, students can identify the limitations of theories. This enables them to test both the hypotheses generated by these theories and the conclusions drawn from experiments suggested by the models. In this chapter, students will have the opportunity to create a diverse range of models to describe scientific concepts. The activities also provide an excellent opportunity for students to reflect on their work in order to attempt to improve their models.

TOPIC 1 Evaluating models in biology

In this topic, we look at examples of the use of models in biology, evaluate their strengths and limitations and consider how to revise models as understanding improves. Students will create models of body shapes and model the process of evolution by repeatedly applying a selection pressure to successive generations of body shape. They will use physical models of animal and plant cells and tissue to model how materials move into and out of cells in the process of osmosis. They will also understand what computer modelling is and what it can do.

Before asking students to evaluate models, ensure that they understand the nature and purpose of models as tools to illustrate, predict and explain a system or phenomena. Discuss with students a variety of simple models to demonstrate that models are representations that explain key observable features of a system. Suitable simple models include the particle model of matter or a food web model. Models should make testable predictions about a scientific theory. This means it is possible to test models against experimental data, and refine the model.

This topic will help promote critical thinking and some of the skills of scientific investigations including interpreting data, explaining results using scientific reasoning, evaluating the validity of a model and explaining improvements or extensions.

Students should have prior knowledge of evolution by natural selection, of diffusion, osmosis and concentration of solutions, and cell membrane structure.

⊂⊃ WEB LINKS

Computer simulations are a form of modelling. On the PBS website there is a simulation of the research done on wild guppies (fish) by Professor John Endler in Trinidad in the 1970s: www.pbs.org/wgbh/evolution/educators/lessons/lesson4/act2.html. The guppies live in small streams or pools. They vary from being brightly coloured to drab. Coloration in males determines attractiveness to females. In different streams and pools, the fish are exposed to a variety of predators. In the simulation, you can collect data, formulate a hypothesis and run a series of experiments.

Activity 1 Modelling evolution by natural selection

This useful activity offers students the opportunity to design data tables, make measurements, test hypotheses, draw conclusions and evaluate models.

Students will naturally start with streamlined shapes. It will work better if they are asked to generate random shapes with the 10 samples for the first trial. The samples should have the same starting mass. At the stage of eliminating the slowest shapes, duplicates should be made of the fastest models to carry out replicates. Drawings of the successful shapes can be assessed by asking other students to re-create the shapes based on the drawings.

 **DP LINKS**

In Topic 5 of the DP biology course, students examine the theory of evolution by natural selection.

QUICK THINK

Both models are idealized simplified representations of the natural world as natural selection occurs in the context of ecosystems. Both models are analogies of natural systems and so will allow predictions and will behave in accordance with what the theory of natural selection predicts. The flashy fish algorithm is programmed to behave in accordance to the theory.

 Activity 2 Modelling movement across a cell membrane

This activity allows students to look at the function of cellular membranes in regulating movement of materials in and out of cells.

[SAFETY]

Students should avoid skin contact with Benedict's solution, especially when heated, and wear eye protection. They should not drink or taste the cola.

This experiment provides practice in making predictions and formulating a testable hypothesis using correct scientific reasoning, in addition to evaluating the limitations of a model. Teachers should point out that much of the behaviour of the molecules that are moving is the actual processes of diffusion and osmosis that occurs in cells. It is the dialysis tubing that is the model being explored.

Phosphoric acid will diffuse through the membrane so a drop in the pH of the water surrounding the tubing should be detected. Fructose can pass through the membrane, so a positive Benedict's test will occur using the water surrounding the tubing. Caramel cannot pass out, so it is predicted that water will be drawn into the tube. The dilution of the caramel will lead to a lighter colour, but no caramel pigment should be detected outside the tubing.

 Activity 3 Modelling osmosis in plant tissues

[SAFETY]

Students should take great care when using the knife or scalpel as their fingers will be very close to the blade. They should not eat or taste the grapes or honey.

This experiment allows students to make predictions and observations. Before students begin this activity, they should be familiar with the terms flaccid and turgid, as well as the process of osmosis.

The grape in distilled water will become turgid. The grape in the 50/50 solution should be slightly flaccid and the grape in the pure honey will lose significant mass and will be highly flaccid.

The changes are due to osmosis. The 50/50 solution and the pure honey solution are hypertonic relative to the grape cube so water will pass out of the grape tissue. The distilled water is hypotonic relative to the grape cube and so water will enter the cube.

Unlike earlier models in the topic, the grape cubes use biological tissue to model osmosis. This has the advantage of being a real biological system but students will need to recognize that a tissue is not a single cell.

Activity 4 **Modelling osmosis in animal tissues**

[SAFETY]

Students should wear eye protection and wash their hands after handling raw eggs.

This experiment allows further exploration of osmosis in a biological tissue. Students will need to create a data table in advance of the experiment. They can gain practice in forming hypotheses, making measurements, organizing data, processing data and evaluating models.

It is expected that the de-shelled egg left in distilled water will gain mass while the eggs left in the salt solution will lose mass. Interestingly, the egg left in the 20% salt solution can be then left in distilled water leading to the flaccid egg becoming turgid. The egg in 10% solution is expected to lose about 25% of its mass.

Further exploration

The same egg can be reused for different concentrations.

Salt concentration g per litre	Estimated per cent change in mass
0.0	+ 8.0%
10.0	+3.0%
20.0	+1.0%
30.0	−3.0%
40.0	−7.0%
50.0	−10.8%

TOPIC 2 Models of atomic structure

The details of many aspects of the structure of the inside of an atom still remain a mystery. However, what we do know about atomic structure has led to many new theories and discoveries in chemistry. Models of the atom are continually being updated and fine-tuned. Although many newer discoveries and additions to the modern atomic structure have occurred since the Bohr model in 1913, students will end their exploration into atomic structure at this point. Understanding atomic structure allows chemists to develop new substances, and also offers a chance to explain chemical and physical properties of substances.

In this topic, students will investigate how flaws in the various models of the atom allowed scientists to introduce updated and more accurate models. They will also learn how line spectra allowed Bohr to put forward his model of the atom. Students will apply their mathematical skills by calculating relative atomic masses.

Ensure that students are familiar with different elements of the periodic table, how to work with percentages and how the wavelength of light relates to its frequency.

QUICK THINK

The discovery of subatomic particles meant that Dalton's assumption that "atoms are indestructible and unchangeable" was incorrect. Additionally, his assumption that "elements are characterized by the mass of their atoms" is also not true—we know isotopes exist. Finding these assumptions to be wrong allowed scientists like Chadwick, Thomson and Rutherford to propose new models of atomic structure.

 Activity 5 | ## Bohr model of the atom and line spectra

In this activity students will observe both continuous and line spectra and use their knowledge of atomic structure to explain line spectra.

Much of what we know about the atomic structure is associated with the Bohr model of the atom. This activity helps explain the energy level aspect of Bohr's model.

By using a gas discharge tube apparatus, a fine diffracting grating of around 600 lines per millimetre and darkroom, students will be able to see the line spectra (emission) of different gases. Use whatever discharge tubes you have available (bromine, chlorine, neon, argon, krypton, mercury vapour, hydrogen).

This activity works best as a whole-class activity with each student recording his or her own observations.

WEB LINKS
If materials are not available, this activity can be replaced with an online simulation. To access the simulation, go to "simulations" and then "emission" on the website:
http://phys.educ.ksu.edu/

QUICK THINK

Scientists can identify the chemical makeup of the atmosphere of stars through the examination of the line spectra observed.

TEACHING IDEA 1
Students can research the importance of the use of other models in chemistry. Do these models have similarities? Are these models agreed on by the scientific community? What is the process through which models become outdated and are modified?

Activity 6 Mapping the inside of an atom

Before you begin this activity, you will need to discuss where to find the atomic number and atomic mass number on the periodic table and the difference between atoms and ions.

The solutions are shown in red in the table below.

Symbol for element or ion	Atomic number	Mass number	Number of protons	Number of electrons	Number of neutrons
Bi	83	209	83	83	126
Pt	78	195	78	78	117
Ir	77	192	77	77	115
Ra	88	226	88	88	138
Xe	54	131	54	54	77
V	23	51	23	23	28
Al	13	27	13	13	14
Es	99	252	99	99	153
Os	76	190	76	76	114
Sn	50	119	50	50	69
Ag	47	108	47	47	61
I	53	127	53	53	74
Ar	18	40	18	18	22
W	74	184	74	74	110
Cs	55	133	55	55	78
Tb	65	159	65	65	94
Tc	43	98	43	43	55
Cu^{2+}	29	64	29	27	35
S^{2-}	16	32	18	16	16
Cl^{-}	17	35	18	17	18
Hg^{2+}	80	201	80	78	121
Ti^{2+}	22	48	22	20	26
Br^{-}	35	80	35	36	45
S^{2-}	16	32	16	18	16
Au^{+}	79	197	79	78	118
F^{-}	9	19	9	10	10
Zn^{2+}	35	65	35	33	30
Cu^{2+}	29	64	29	27	35
O^{2-}	8	16	8	10	8

One of the flaws with Dalton's model of the atom was that he assumed all atoms of each element were exactly the same. We now know this is not true due to the existence of isotopes.

 **DP LINKS**
This activity links with Topic 2 in DP chemistry where students will investigate how the mass spectrometer is used to determine the relative atomic mass of an element from its isotopic composition and solve abundance of isotopes calculations.

 Activity 7 **Isotopes—Beanium lab**

You will need to make a sample of "beanium" for use in this experiment — using a combination of different dried beans (kidney beans, chickpeas, black-eyed peas and brown lentils) that can be easily separated from one another. Use at least three different types of bean. Each group will need a sample size of about 150 cm^3, the mass of which will depend on the beans you use. Make sure students allow for the mass of the container (eg paper cup) they use to contain the beans when using the digital balance.

The data table that students design should contain at least the following collected data:

Total mass of sample (g)				
	Isotope 1	Isotope 2	Isotope 3	Isotope ...
Number of atoms of this isotope				
Mass of isotope (g)				

Students' answers to the questions will depend on the specific sample that each group receives. Students' answers will not be whole numbers, and they should not round calculations too early. It would be good for all groups in the class to compare their calculated relative atomic mass. Students' answers could all be different because their samples have slightly different abundances due to the random sampling from the larger container you provide.

Answers

a) 12.01
b) 14.00
c) 24.32
d) 29.28
e) 95.98

DP LINKS
As with the previous activity, this activity links with Topic 2 in DP chemistry where students will investigate how the mass spectrometer is used to determine the relative atomic mass of an element from its isotopic composition and solve abundance of isotopes calculations.

TOPIC 3 Making waves

In this topic, students study the characteristics of waves. Inquiry-based activities will demonstrate to students how the behaviour of waves can be modelled. From this, the relationship between speed, frequency and wavelength is derived.

Students will discuss how, by using models of waves, earthquakes can be explained and perhaps predicted. Advances in technology will also be studied (eg noise-cancelling headphones have been developed from an understanding of interference of waves).

Visualization of how energy is transferred from one place to another is helpful. Activities in this topic are centred on deducing the properties of waves through modelling them with a slinky. It is important to stress to students that the relationships that they derive in their investigations are true for all transverse or longitudinal waves.

⊖ WEB LINKS

Discussing these articles with students may help them with Activity 8.

http://sciencenetlinks.com/science-news/science-updates/predicting-earthquakes/

http://mpe2013.org/2013/03/11/modeling-and-prediction-of-earthquakes/

www.bbc.co.uk/science/earth/natural_disasters/earthquake#p00gmsgt

www.cbsnews.com/news/are-scientists-getting-closer-to-predicting-major-earthquakes/

http://earthquake.usgs.gov/learn/publications/saferstructures/

QUICK THINK

Monitoring methods to look for:

- small ground displacements at a fault boundary (eg using GPS) that may indicate the strain is starting to be released
- detection of smaller earthquakes that might indicate a fault is about to slip
- a seismic gap (the absence of normal seismicity in an area for a long period)
- strain rate changes using a strain sensor.

Other methods include:

- detecting anomalies of the ground electric field (due to squeezing rock under high pressures)
- observations of groundwater level change
- detecting increases in radon gas (thought to released from fault zones prior to slipping).

Activity 8 \ Modelling transverse waves

This activity allows students to visualize what is meant by a wave (they can see energy moving through the slinky) and the difference between a transverse and longitudinal wave. Students will investigate the relationship between the amplitude and speed of a transverse wave.

In preparation for this activity, spend time explaining to students the differences between a transverse and longitudinal wave. Students should understand the terms amplitude, wavelength, frequency and speed, oscillation, period, rest point.

For homework, students should graph their results and state whether there is a relationship between amplitude and the speed of a transverse wave, using the data they have collected.

Further exploration

To delve into this topic more deeply, students could find out the relationship between the energy carried in a wave and the amplitude of a wave. To do this, ask students to transfer different amounts of kinetic energy to a wave on the Slinky (larger hand movements to make wave) and observe the amplitude. Students should find that as the energy carried in the wave increases, the amplitude increases. Amplitude is proportional to energy.

TIP

If students are struggling to understand the difference between transverse and longitudinal waves, a quick activity is to give students a piece of rope, dominoes and a slinky. Ask students to "push" energy through each of these and record the direction of motion.

Activity 9 Modelling wave interference

This activity helps students visualize and understand interference.

In preparation for this activity, ask students to discuss why a concert in a hall with good acoustics produces a much louder sound than a concert in a hall with bad acoustics, even though the instruments are exactly the same and played in the same way.

For homework, students should complete the diagrams and discuss what each diagram shows.

TEACHING IDEA 2

Another method to teach interference is to use the PhET wave on a string simulation at http://phet.colorado.edu/en/simulation/wave-on-a-string.

This simulation is a rope on the ground that is being wiggled from side to side at one end, so that a wave propagates along the rope. Students can change the frequency and the amplitude of the wave. Students can investigate other properties of the wave such as tension and damping. This activity can be linked to the standing waves topic in Chapter 14 on patterns.

Guiding questions:

1) What are the characteristics of waves?

2) What is amplitude? What is tension? What is damping?

3) How does the amplitude of wiggling affect the speed of the wave?

4) Are the waves in the simulation transverse or longitudinal?

5) How do waves behave differently with free and fixed ends?

 Activity 10 Exploring wave speed

This activity consolidates students' understanding of the relationships between properties of transverse or longitudinal waves. It allows students to develop their investigative and analytical techniques.

In preparation for this activity, make students aware of the properties of waves and the wave equation. They should also be aware of the equipment available for their investigation.

For homework, students should write a full report on their investigation. This report should include:

- their research question
- hypothesis with scientific explanation
- variables to be measured, with correct units
- equipment list and drawing of equipment set-up
- method in enough detail that someone else could follow it
- table of results with correct units of measurement
- examples of how results were calculated
- conclusion
- evaluation
- suggested improvements.

DP LINKS

In DP physics, students must:

- explain the motion of particles of a medium when a wave passes through it for both transverse and longitudinal cases
- sketch and interpret displacement–distance graphs and displacement–time graphs for transverse and longitudinal waves
- solve problems involving wave speed, frequency and wavelength
- investigate the speed of sound experimentally.

CHAPTER LINKS

Chapter 14 on patterns further develops students' understanding of waves, in particular the properties of interference and how interference can be used to explain standing waves.

Summary

In this chapter, students have investigated a variety of models to represent different scientific theories. During their investigations, they will have learned how to represent patterns of observations as simplified models and the usefulness of such models for explaining scientific phenomena. This is especially true when the scale of measurement or volume of data makes visualization difficult. As a result, their understanding of the relationships between variables will have been enhanced, providing them with the skills required to produce their own models. By constantly evaluating models and their use, students will have developed critical and analytical skills, enabling them to appreciate the value and limitations of using models in science.

CHAPTER 9 Interaction

	ATL skills	Science skills
TOPIC 1 Interactions between organisms		
Activity 1 Forming a hypothesis about the variables affecting herbivore damage	✓ Make guesses, ask "what if" questions and generate testable hypotheses.	✓ Formulate a testable hypothesis and explain it using scientific reasoning. ✓ Design a method for testing a hypothesis, explaining how to manipulate the variables and how data will be collected.
Activity 2 Investigating the effect of conifers on other plants' growth	✓ Make guesses, ask "what if" questions and generate testable hypotheses.	✓ Formulate a testable hypothesis and explain it using scientific reasoning. ✓ Design a method for testing a hypothesis, explaining how to manipulate the variables and how data will be collected. ✓ Organize and present data in tables ready for processing.
Activity 3 Strategies for removing biofilms	✓ Collect and analyse data to identify solutions and make informed decisions.	✓ Interpret data to draw justifiable conclusions.
TOPIC 2 Chemical bonding		
Activity 4 Chemical bonds	✓ Draw reasonable conclusions and generalizations.	✓ Use appropriate scientific conventions to visually represent abstract ideas.
Activity 5 Physical properties of covalent and ionic compounds	✓ Draw reasonable conclusions and generalizations.	✓ Organize and present data in tables ready for processing. ✓ Interpret data to draw justifiable conclusions.
Activity 6 Constructing molecular models	✓ Make connections between various sources of information.	✓ Use appropriate scientific conventions to visually represent abstract ideas.
Activity 7 Bonding continuum	✓ Present information in a variety of formats and platforms.	✓ Organize and present information using appropriate scientific terminology.
TOPIC 3 Electromagnetism		
Activity 8 Exploring magnetic interactions	✓ Collect, record and verify data.	✓ Use appropriate scientific conventions to visually represent abstract ideas.

Activity 9 Creating an electromagnet	✓ Design new machines, media and technologies.	✓ Interpret data to draw justifiable conclusions.
Activity 10 Electromagnet inquiry	✓ Gather and organize relevant information to formulate an argument.	✓ Formulate a testable hypothesis and explain it using scientific reasoning.
		✓ Design a method for testing a hypothesis, explaining how to manipulate the variables and how data will be collected.
		✓ Organize and present data in tables ready for processing.
		✓ Interpret data to draw justifiable conclusions.
		✓ Organize and present information using appropriate scientific terminology.
		✓ Describe improvements to a method, to reduce sources of error.

Introducing interaction

Interactions are constantly occurring between all aspects of the world. By observing the consequences of these interactions, students can make predictions about future interactions and create models to represent how systems actually work. In this chapter, students will investigate the interactions of organisms, atoms, ions or molecules and magnetic forces. They will also investigate how a change in one aspect of a system influences the other components directly or indirectly.

To help students identify exact associations between entities, activities emphasize the need to identify and control variables so that a specific interaction can be observed. This is supplemented by highlighting the use of modelling or graphical representation of ideas. Allowing students to transform their knowledge into other forms can help eradicate misconceptions and also provide them with a system within which they can structure their knowledge. When they subsequently investigate an interaction within a system, students can refer to their model to help with a logical, scientific approach to predicting and explaining observations.

TOPIC 1 Interactions between organisms

In this topic we study the interactions of organisms and the effects of those interactions on other components in a system. Students will investigate herbivore–plant interactions, how allelopathic interactions affect species survival and how physical factors such as brushing disturb the interactions between dental bacteria and teeth substrate.

Students will develop their skills in forming hypotheses using scientific explanations and designing an investigation to test a hypothesis.

Activity 1   Forming a hypothesis about the variables affecting herbivore damage

Stage 1 of the unit planner

Key concept	Related concept(s)	Global context
Systems	Interaction	Orientation in time and place
Statement of inquiry		
The degree of predation of a leaf depends on predator preference and leaf variation.		

One variable that could be investigated is leaf shape for a single species of plant. For example, some variants of the popular garden plant morning glory, *Ipomoea* sp, produce two types of leaf, heart-shaped and lobed. One possible hypothesis is: If a sample of morning glory leaves that have been predated by herbivores is examined, then a greater percentage of the original surface area of a lobe-shaped leaf will have been consumed because for the same surface it has less surface in contact with edges.

Assessment

If you choose to assess students on this task, you can use criterion B. The task-specific descriptor in the top band (7–8) should read that students are able to:

- explain the reasons why the dependent variable (such as leaf area) is affected by the independent variable and the reasons why their research question is significant
- formulate and explain a testable hypothesis using correct scientific reasoning
- explain how to monitor and control other variables that might affect leaf predation (such as plant growth conditions, age of leaf, insect species), and explain how sufficient, relevant data will be collected including how the dependent variable (such as mean leaf area consumed) is measured
- design a logical, complete and safe method in which they select appropriate materials and equipment, for example to measure surface area and percentage area predated.

TIP

Surface area can be measured by tracing the leaf on an erasable clear plastic grid or by taking a photo and analysing it using image processing software.

Activity 2   Investigating the effect of conifers on other plants' growth

In this activity students will design an experiment to investigate the effect of conifers on germinating seeds.

Stage 1 of the unit planner

Key concept	Related concept(s)	Global context
Systems	Interaction	Orientation in time and place
Statement of inquiry		
Species that live in the same ecosystem and compete for the same resources will interact to ensure adequate resources for their offspring.		

When an organism produces a chemical to influence the survival or reproduction of another species, this is known as allelopathy. In step 1, students are asked to explain why needles from different seasons might differ in the effect. This would be the case if the allelopathic chemical degraded with time.

[SAFETY]

Students should wash their hands after making and using the extract.

TIP

Recommended plant seeds for this activity are radish and watercress.

WEB LINKS

A detailed protocol for an experiment like this can be found at: www.saps.org.uk.
Search for "inhibitory effects of conifers".

Assessment

If you choose to assess students on this task, you can use criterion B and criterion C. The task-specific descriptor in the top band (7–8) should read that students are able to:

Criterion B

- explain why other plants' growth might be affected by the conifer extract
- formulate and explain a testable hypothesis regarding the impact of the extract on percent germination using correct scientific reasoning
- explain how to manipulate the independent variable and how the other variables that could affect the seed germination or growth will be controlled (including a control experiment with sterile water), and explain how sufficient, relevant data will be collected (including repeats and calculation of mean)
- design a logical, complete and safe method in which they select appropriate materials and equipment.

Criterion C

- correctly collect data, and organize, transform and present the percentage of germinated (or inhibited) seeds in numerical and visual forms
- accurately interpret data and explain the percentage germination results using correct scientific reasoning
- evaluate the validity of a hypothesis based on the outcome of the scientific investigation
- evaluate the validity of the method based on the outcome of their investigation, identifying limitations and discussing their implications for the results
- explain improvements or extensions to the method that would benefit the scientific investigation.

Further exploration

Tests could also be performed to see if the extract has antibacterial properties (inhibits microbial growth). The area of the zone of inhibition could be measured.

 Activity 3 Strategies for removing biofilms

In this activity students will investigate the factors favouring the removal of plaque, modelling plaque on teeth using a layer of soft cheese on a rough surface.

Biofilms are found in many places. For example, in an aquarium, the slime covering the tubing to the air filter represents a biofilm.

Some students may think they are removing a biofilm when they are removing the cheese. Emphasize that the cheese is a model of a biofilm, and that they are investigating strategies for the removal of plaque.

[SAFETY]

Students should not taste or eat the cheese. They should not put disclosing tablets in their mouths during this activity.

TEACHING IDEA 1

Exploring biofilms is an important aspect of understanding the key concept of systems as the biofilm represents an emergent property of the bacterial system.

When many individual organisms interact, new patterns or properties are often observed as a consequence of the interactions. Properties that are properties of the collective rather than properties of individuals are called emergent properties. The coordinated movement of a flock of birds or a school of fish is an example of an emergent property.

⟳ WEB LINKS

The Game of Life is a simulation that allows you to manipulate variables impacting the reproduction of squares and then observe the emergence of patterns and properties that are the outcome of the interaction of the individual squares. Go to www.bitstorm.org/gameoflife/

Further exploration

The disclosing tablets can be used to view plaque formations on students' teeth. One possible experiment would involve applying the tablets over a series of days to determine if brushing patterns can reduce the amount of plaque.

Chemical bonding

This topic will help students develop an understanding of the interactions that take place at the atomic level and that explain chemical bonding. Students will focus on the related concept of interaction by studying chemical bonding and structure. Specifically, students will investigate how atoms bond to form either ionic or covalent compounds. They will consider how metallic bonds form, and will distinguish ionic and covalent compounds by their physical properties. Students will examine 3-D molecular model representations and consider bonding as a continuum rather than as separate types of bonding. Students will develop skills of explanation, basic laboratory techniques, spatial awareness and the ability to draw 3-D molecules.

Students should have prior knowledge of atomic structure, the understanding that electrons orbit an atom's nucleus, and have basic knowledge of electron configuration.

 Activity 4 **Chemical bonds**

This introductory activity requires students to explain how interactions between adjacent atoms cause covalent and ionic bonds to form. The covalent and ionic bonds are represented in diagrams. This ensures that students develop a strong grasp of the idea of covalent and ionic bonding. They begin by explaining a simple single covalent bond and progress to a double bond and then to explain the formation of an ammonia molecule and sodium chloride.

Students can get into pairs to share explanations after the activity.

H–H molecule

- There are two hydrogen atoms, each with one electron and a positive nucleus.
- The negative electron in each hydrogen atom is attracted to the positive nucleus of the other hydrogen atom.
- The end result is that the two hydrogen atoms share two electrons and, therefore, are joined in a covalent bond.

O=O molecule

- There are two oxygen atoms, each with two single electrons in the outer electron shell and a positive nucleus.
- The negative electrons in each oxygen atom are attracted to the positive nucleus of the other oxygen atom.
- The end result is that the two oxygen atoms share two pairs (four) of electrons and, therefore, are joined in a double covalent bond.

Ammonia molecule

- There is a hydrogen atom that has one electron and a positive nucleus. There is a nitrogen atom that has three single electrons and a pair of electrons and a positive nucleus.
- The negative electron in the hydrogen atom is attracted to the positive nucleus of the nitrogen atom, while the negative electron of the nitrogen atom is attracted to the positive nucleus of the hydrogen atom. However, the nitrogen atom still has two single electrons.
- In order to pair up the two remaining single electrons in the nitrogen atoms, two more hydrogens are needed.
- The final structure will contain three hydrogen atoms and one nitrogen atom. There are three separate pairs of electrons shared between the nitrogen atom and the three hydrogen atoms.

NaCl

- The sodium ion has one "extra" electron in its third energy level, while the chlorine atom is one electron away from having its 3p shell full.
- The sodium atom has lost an electron and has become a positively charged sodium ion. The chlorine atom has gained an electron from the sodium atom to become a chloride ion. The chloride ion now has a full outer shell (all the outer shell electrons are paired).

⊂⊃ DP LINKS

In Topic 4 in DP chemistry, students will further investigate covalent bonds and covalent structures during which they will use the VSEPR theory to explain shapes of covalent compounds.

Activity 5 Physical properties of covalent and ionic compounds

This activity allows students to investigate what influence covalent and ionic bonds have on the properties of each type of substance. The conclusions that students should come to are as follows.

- You can smell the odour of covalent compounds more easily than ionic compounds.
- Ionic compounds are harder than covalent compounds.
- Ionic compounds have a higher melting point than covalent compounds.
- Ionic compounds are more readily soluble in water than covalent compounds.
- Ionic compounds when dissolved in distilled water conduct electricity, while covalent compounds do not.

If you do not have access to camphor, substitute a sample of a non-toxic covalent compound that could be used to test the same properties. If your school does not have a conductivity meter, you can make use of a simple circuit with a battery and 1.5 V bulb.

[SAFETY]

- Students should wear eye protection and wash their hands after handling the chemicals.
- Ensure students heat the camphor for less than 30 seconds. If it ignites, students should stop heating and cover the beaker with a bench mat.
- For any substituted substance that is toxic, check the MSDS sheet to see whether students can handle the substance or should wear gloves. Having students rub the substances between their fingers can be replaced by trying to crush the substance between a spatula and a watch glass.
- Ensure that you instruct students on the correct technique for wafting odours. A video demonstrating the correct technique is noted in web links.

TIP

Ensure that you correct students if they describe one type of bond as being "stronger" than another. The observations of many of these experiments, although rooted in the type of bonding, are also dependent on intermolecular forces.

DP LINKS

This activity links with Topic 4 in DP chemistry, in which students will examine in more depth the properties of ionic compounds as well as use intermolecular forces to explain the properties of covalent compounds.

WEB LINKS

To ensure that students properly smell for odours go to the site below and then search for "How to safely smell a liquid": www.youtube.com

 Activity 6 Constructing molecular models

One of the most difficult ideas in chemistry for students to clearly understand is how to use their knowledge of interactions/chemical bonds to explain how molecules are formed. The use of molecular model kits helps students to visualize how atoms are connected to form molecules.

This activity can be done in small groups if the number of molecular model kits available is low. Students will find that if you bond the same atoms together in different ways and with different numbers you make different molecules (ethane, ethyne, benzene). They will also find that because an atom of carbon can make four bonds, it can produce a very large variety of compounds.

WEB LINKS

If your school does not have molecular model kits you can do this online. For example, the molecular model-building website at PhET: http://phet.colorado.edu/en/simulation/build-a-molecule

Answers

- H_2, Cl_2, Br_2, HCl and HBr

All bonds formed are single bonds; all compounds formed are linear in shape.

- methane (CH_4) and carbon tetrachloride (CCl_4)

All bonds formed are single bonds (there will be four of them); both shapes that students will see are tetrahedral, however they will use different terms to explain this shape.

■ ammonia (NH_3)

All bonds formed will be single bonds; the shape will look like a pyramid with a hole on top of the nitrogen. The proper name for this shape is trigonal pyramidal.

■ water (H_2O)

All bonds formed will be single, with two empty holes on the central oxygen atom. The shape is described as bent.

■ oxygen (O_2), carbon dioxide (CO_2) and ethene (C_2H_4)

All three compounds will contain a double bond and ethene will also contain two single bonds between the C and H. The shape that will be seen is linear in all three compounds.

■ nitrogen (N_2), hydrogen cyanide (HCN) and ethyne (C_2H_2)

All three compounds will contain a triple bond and hydrogen cyanide and ethyne will also contain single bonds between the C and H. The shape that will be seen is linear in all three compounds.

■ ethanoic acid/vinegar (CH_3COOH)

The shapes that this molecule has are tetrahedral, trigonal planar and bent (Figure 9.1).

■ benzene (C_6H_6)

Benzene contains alternating single and double bonds between the six carbon atoms, which are arranged in a ring with each carbon atom having one singly bonded hydrogen atom. The shape is trigonal planar around each carbon atom (Figure 9.2).

DP LINKS

In Topic 4 in DP chemistry, students will further investigate covalent bonds and covalent structures during which they will use the VSEPR theory to explain shapes of covalent compounds.

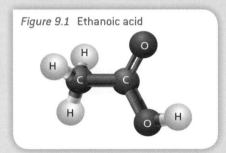
Figure 9.1 Ethanoic acid

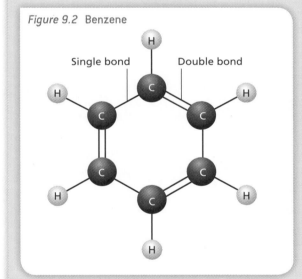
Figure 9.2 Benzene

Single bond   Double bond

TIP

To help students draw models in three dimensions you may want to introduce the idea of a dotted line for atoms that are going away from the reader and the idea of a wedge to represent atoms that are coming towards the reader. A solid line can be used to represent bonds that are on the same plane. An example is shown in Figure 9.3.

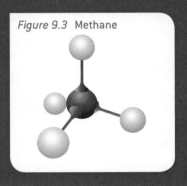
Figure 9.3 Methane

Further exploration

You could also encourage the students to develop different models of the interactions between atoms in a molecule. Students are given or choose a molecule which they must represent in a model of their choice, using whatever materials they wish. However, they cannot use molecular model kits.

Activity 7   Bonding continuum

This activity will test students about their understanding of bonding, which has so far been explained rather simply. Covalent and ionic bonds are actually two points on a continuum of bonding rather than two different types of bonding. Encourage students to explore as many different combinations of interactions between atoms as possible. The number of combinations of interactions with a zero difference in electronegativity (100% covalent) is very small compared to the number of combinations of interactions with greater than a zero difference in electronegativity.

Alternatives to the classification system of interactions that are present in chemical bonds could be brainstormed and the merit of each alternative discussed in class.

Encourage students to really think about and comment on the statement "scientific concepts do not cover all possibilities and should not be considered truth". Revisiting this statement throughout the course would allow students to really consider the science they are learning.

DP LINKS
This activity links with TOK and the natural sciences way of knowing.

WEB LINKS
Provide students with a table of electronegativities. Such a table can be found at www.sciencegeek.net/tables/

TOPIC 3   Electromagnetism

In this topic, students will explore how magnets interact with each other. Students will develop their understanding of the applications of magnetic fields in technology, for example MagLev trains. Other activities in this topic are centred on investigating the interactions between electric and magnetic fields. From this, the generation of electricity can be further understood.

WEB LINKS
Clips 26–30 at the website below are short videos that discuss the theory that cows align themselves with the Earth's magnetic field: www.bbc.co.uk/schools/teachers/bang/videos/lesson10_sampling_techniques.shtml

TEACHING IDEA 2
To capture students' interest and introduce the concept of magnetic materials, describe the "cow magnet". Tell students that cows often have a magnet placed into one of their stomachs. This is so that all the iron or steel that cows may accidently eat (nails, staples, bits of wire) can be collected in one place. This metal could otherwise puncture the stomach lining, damaging the surrounding organs and causing irritation and inflammation, known as hardware disease.

You could also look at the idea that cows tend to align themselves along the Earth's magnetic field, facing either magnetic north or south.

Activity 8 Exploring magnetic interactions

This activity demonstrates to students the properties of a magnet. It allows students to visualize *why* magnets can interact with each other. Before students start this activity, they should understand that magnets can attract and repel other magnetic materials. Students should also know what materials are magnetic.

Students might find it difficult to understand what is meant by question b) "What direction do you think these field lines "flow" in?" You should explain that scientists define the direction of a magnetic field as being the direction of the force that would be exerted on a north magnetic pole in the magnetic field. This means that the direction of the field is easily found by noting the direction that the south-seeking end of a compass points. If you put your compass near the north magnetic pole of your bar magnet, marked with N, the north-seeking end of the compass points away from the pole.

In their conclusion, students should note that the field lines represent the area in which the magnetic force from the magnetic field is felt (the field is in three dimensions although students only plot the field in the horizontal plane). They should also note that the distance or separation between the magnetic field lines represents the strength of the magnetic field. The field of a bar magnet is strongest at the poles, where the field line density is greatest.

Further exploration

Students could join with another group to investigate the interaction of more than two magnets in a configuration of their choosing. They should use larger sheets of paper if they are considering this, to avoid getting iron filings on the magnets.

⊂⊃ WEB LINKS

This link can be used to show students the orientation and direction of a magnetic field. Students can also use this simulation to investigate the factors that affect the strength of an electromagnet:

http://phet.colorado.edu/en/simulation/magnets-and-electromagnets

 Activity 9 Creating an electromagnet

Students will learn how to create a magnetic field by using an electric current. They can test the strength of the magnetic field by counting the number of paper clips held by the electromagnet. The wire should preferably be a heavy gauge >12.

[SAFETY]

The electromagnet should be disconnected when the measurements have been taken as the coil of wire will get hot enough to burn if it is left connected.

Students should observe that when the circuit is connected and a nail or paper clip is held nearby, the object vibrates, or gets pulled into the coil. The electromagnet will not pick up paper clips when the circuit is disconnected—that is, an electromagnet can be switched on and off.

Students can explore varying the design of the electromagnet by changing the number of coils around the nail and using a different number of batteries. Students understand that more coils around the nail and/or more cells increases the magnetic force (shown by being able to pick up more paper clips). They will investigate one of these factors more quantitatively in Activity 10 where they should consider the current in the coiled wire, not just the number of cells/batteries.

Further exploration

Ask students to research one way in which the use of electromagnets has advanced technology (such as headphones, loudspeakers, MagLev trains).

Activity 10 Electromagnet inquiry

Stage 1 of the unit planner

Key concept	Related concept(s)	Global context
Relationship	Interaction	Scientific and technical innovation
Statement of inquiry		
The relationship between fields can cause interactions that have helped promote technical innovation.		

🔗 **WEB LINKS**
If students need further guidance on how to set up their electromagnet they can search "how to make an electromagnet" at www.teachertube.com

This activity allows students to investigate the factors that affect the strength of an electromagnet. It also allows them to take further what they discovered in Activity 9, by measuring in a more systematic way (you should provide ammeters) and plotting a graph to identify the relationship between the variables. Students could also consider adding cores made from different materials. Before they begin this activity, you should recap with students how an electromagnet is made and what a magnetic field is.

[SAFETY]

Ensure the voltage of the battery/low voltage power supply is kept below 6 V. Higher voltages can cause dangerous overheating of the coil. A "Westminster pattern" very low voltage supply is best.

The electromagnet should be disconnected when the measurements have been taken as the coil of wire will get hot enough to burn if left connected.

For homework, students will write a full scientific lab report on this investigation.

Assessment

If you choose to assess students on this task, you can use criterion B or C. The task-specific descriptor in the top band (7–8) should read that students are able to:

Criterion B

- explain a factor that affects an electromagnet and how they will test it by a scientific investigation
- formulate and explain a hypothesis for testing a factor that affects an electromagnet, using correct scientific reasoning
- explain how to manipulate and control the variables, and explain how sufficient, relevant data will be collected by selecting at least five values of the independent variable and checking reproducibility of results
- design a logical, complete and safe method in which they select appropriate materials and equipment, such as an ammeter to measure current, and show an awareness of the hazards from the hot coil.

Criterion C

- organize results in a suitable table, process data (calculating mean of repeat readings) and correctly present processed data as a scatter graph to aid understanding of the results
- accurately interpret data and explain results using correct scientific reasoning
- evaluate the validity of their hypothesis based on the results they collected
- evaluate the validity of the method based on the outcome of their investigation, for example whether paper clips gave a valid measure of the electromagnet's strength

🔗 **DP LINKS**
- TOK: Field patterns provide a visualization of a complex phenomenon, essential to an understanding of this topic. Why might it be useful to regard knowledge in a similar way, using the metaphor of knowledge as a map—a simplified representation of reality?
- In DP physics students study magnetic fields and force in detail. Students must be able to sketch and interpret magnetic field patterns.
- In DP physics students determine the direction of the magnetic field based on current direction.
- In DP physics students solve problems involving magnetic forces, fields, current and charges.

🔗 **INTERDISCIPLINARY LINKS**
In Individuals and Societies students study sustainable energy. Renewable energy sources can be used to generate electricity due to the interaction between magnetic and electric fields, in the same way that fossil fuel and nuclear power stations generate electricity. The implications of the generation of electricity through renewable sources is also discussed.

- explain how they could improve on their method, for example to improve the method of measurement
- explain an extension to the investigation, using their results to develop a new line of inquiry, for example to investigate anomalies or unexpected results.

Further exploration

- Students can investigate why the number of coils around the nail and the current in the coiled wire have an effect on the strength of the magnetic field.
- The current in the coiled wire can also be affected by the thickness of the conducting material. Students could continue their investigation and determine how the gauge or material of a wire affects the strength of an electromagnet, for the same number of coils and batteries/voltage. Students can be tested by discussing what their results tell them about the resistance in the different wires.

WEB LINKS

Search YouTube using "Magnets: how do they work" and "Electromagnetic induction"
www.youtube.com

TEACHING IDEA 3

Discuss the reflection question: How does an electromagnet differ from a permanent magnet?

In an electromagnet, the charges in motion are in the form of an electric current, which is established by an electric potential difference across the two ends of the wire. In a permanent magnet, nature provides the mechanism for the motion of charge, which is in the form of the spin of an electron and its orbit about the nucleus.

Discuss the reflection question: How could a light bulb that is close to, but not touching, an electromagnet be lit?

The answer is electromagnetic induction. A time-varying magnetic field adjacent to a closed loop of wire will induce current in the loop of wire. If the bulb is part of the circuit (in series with the wire) then current will flow through the bulb and if the current is sufficiently large it will cause the filament to glow.

TEACHING IDEA 4

To develop students' understanding of how the interaction between electricity and a magnetic field generates an induced current, set the following puzzle.

The battery in an electric toothbrush is charged by placing it in a plastic holder, but there are no metal-to-metal contacts. Both toothbrush and the holder have plastic casings. How does the interaction between electric and magnetic fields allow energy to be transferred from the holder to the battery?

The answer is by electromagnetic induction. A time-varying magnetic field is created by a coil (small electromagnet) in the base of the holder. The magnetic field from this coil induces a current in the neighbouring coil that is mounted in the base of the toothbrush. The induced current is then used to charge a battery in the toothbrush.

Summary

The variety and complexity of interactions in science can sometimes prevent understanding of scientific theories. By learning how to isolate and subsequently study interactions, students can start to organize their knowledge into systems that can be manipulated to help further understand a concept.

The activities in this chapter aim to introduce interactions over a range of sizes and timescales and highlight that nothing ever acts independently or in isolation. As a result, students should be aware of confounding variables within an experiment and thus control for these accordingly in their experimental designs.

Consequences

	ATL skills	Science skills
TOPIC 1 Environmental chemistry		
Activity 1 Comparing differences in particulate air pollution	✓ Process data and report results.	✓ Interpret data and explain results using scientific reasoning. ✓ Use appropriate scientific terminology to make the meaning of your findings clear.
Activity 2 Measuring particulates produced by different vehicles	✓ Make guesses, ask "what if" questions and generate testable hypotheses.	✓ Formulate a testable hypothesis using scientific reasoning. ✓ Interpret data and explain results using scientific reasoning. ✓ Describe possible extensions to the method for further inquiry. ✓ Use appropriate scientific terminology to make the meaning of your findings clear.
Activity 3 Electric vehicles—viable or not?	✓ Evaluate and select information sources and digital tools based on their appropriateness to specific tasks.	✓ Critically evaluate information from various sources, demonstrating awareness of limitations, misrepresentation or lack of balance.
Activity 4 Monitoring the effects of acid deposition	✓ Interpret data.	✓ Design a method for testing a hypothesis, explaining how to manipulate variables, and ensure that enough data is collected. ✓ Interpret data and explain results using scientific reasoning. ✓ Describe possible extensions to the method for further inquiry.
TOPIC 2 Effect of increased greenhouse gases on global temperature		
Activity 5 Greenhouse effect in a beaker	✓ Practise observing carefully in order to recognize problems.	✓ Formulate a testable hypothesis using scientific reasoning. ✓ Organize and present data in tables ready for processing. ✓ Interpret data and explain results using scientific reasoning. ✓ Plot scatter graphs with a line of best fit and identify trends. ✓ Describe possible extensions to the method for further inquiry. ✓ Use appropriate scientific terminology to make the meaning of your findings clear.

Activity 6 Interpreting recent data on atmospheric carbon dioxide levels	✓ Interpret data.	✓ Distinguish between correlation and cause and effect. ✓ Interpret data and explain results using scientific reasoning.
Activity 7 Interpreting the change in carbon dioxide in the atmosphere over the past 200 years	✓ Interpret data.	✓ Distinguish between correlation and cause and effect. ✓ Interpret data and explain results using scientific reasoning.

Introducing consequences

Consequences are the observable or measurable effects resulting from earlier events. Consequences can range from small-scale molecular interactions to the global manifestation of climate change. All sciences investigate consequences and the observation of them forms a fundamental component of the scientific method of generating knowledge. This concept is an excellent tool for demonstrating the similarity of approach across the sciences and why disciplines can or cannot be considered scientific.

This chapter focuses directly on the consequences of human activity on the environment, using specific examples to highlight local and global effects. Students will investigate how modelling enables us to make predictions about the consequences of our actions. This knowledge enables us to create solutions to solve these potential problems. This chapter also highlights how knowledge from different sciences needs to be integrated if the models we produce are to be accurate representations and therefore create viable solutions.

Students may have already encountered the idea of consequences in Chapter 3 on change where they investigate the precautionary principle. In this chapter, they will have the opportunity to investigate the direct consequences of human activity in order to generate restorative solutions rather than preventative ones.

This concept is also excellent for integrating the sciences with other disciplines, most notably Individuals and Societies. Students have the opportunity to explore the role and impact of science in society. They will also be able to evaluate a scientific innovation in the context of economic and social development in a variety of different countries.

 **DP LINKS**
The scientific method for the generation of knowledge is what defines science as an area of knowledge within TOK. Students often enjoy discussions about how knowledge is generated in other subject areas. This represents an excellent opportunity to compare and contrast science with other areas of knowledge.

TOPIC 1 # Environmental chemistry

Some consequences of chemical innovation are positive (chemical fertilizers to increase crop yield), but many have had negative consequences for the environment (air pollution from internal combustion engines, acid deposition from industrial processes).

In this topic, students will consider the value and trustworthiness of different sources of information, investigate global particulate air pollution, design an experiment to measure the amount of particulate matter in vehicle exhaust and design an experiment to investigate the effect of acid deposition on marble statues.

Through these activities, students develop the skills of analysing and critiquing different internet sources and designing experiments by examining the variables involved and formulating hypotheses.

Before students examine the phenomenon of environmental chemistry, you will want to ensure that they have prior knowledge of designing experiments including the listing of variables and formulating hypotheses, and a basic understanding of chemical reactions and targeted Internet searches.

 Activity 1 ## Comparing differences in particulate air pollution

Students compare and contrast levels of atmospheric particulate matter in different areas of the world and use Internet sources to investigate what action different local authorities have planned to reduce levels of those particulates. Students will gain an appreciation that governmental reaction to pollution is not uniform across the globe. Some countries are very proactive in developing solutions whereas others, for a variety of reasons, are limited in their reaction to high levels of particulate matter.

More developed countries tend to have lower levels of atmospheric PM10 despite higher per capita use of fossil fuels in transport, energy supply and industrial activity. Factors may include lower population density, cooler climate, greater use of cleaner sources like wind or solar technology, and policies such as car sharing.

Students can do this task individually and then get into pairs to share explanations.

 **DP LINKS**

This activity links with option C in the DP chemistry guide where students will investigate the environmental impact of different energy sources, their impact on global warming and the role that particulates play in this.

 Activity 2 ## Measuring particulates produced by different vehicles

In this activity, students will investigate particulate emission from vehicles and look at how they might develop an anti-idling policy in their schools.

Encourage students to consider different types of vehicles (automobiles, mopeds, hybrid cars, trucks, SUVs, etc), vehicles of different ages and vehicles with and without catalytic converters, if possible.

An example of a simple procedure that students could develop involves finding the mass of a white sports sock or piece of material (this would require a balance with an accuracy of 0.01 g) and enveloping a vehicle's exhaust pipe with it. Turn on the vehicle and run the engine for at least 10 minutes. Wait at least 5 minutes until the exhaust pipe has cooled down and then remove the sock/material and measure its mass again. The difference in mass represents the mass of particulates collected. Variables that students should consider include, but are not limited to, age of vehicle, size of engine in the vehicle, type of fuel the vehicle uses, whether or not a catalytic converter exists, service record of the vehicle, time since engine had previously run, etc.

Further exploration

Students could extend this experiment by determining the type of particulate matter that is collected. To do this, they would carry out chemical identification tests on the particulates.

[SAFETY]

- This experiment should be carried out in a well-ventilated area.
- Students will need to be careful when working around the vehicle's exhaust pipe, which may still be warm if the vehicle has recently been used. Students need to ensure that the exhaust pipe is cool enough to safely work around and should use oven gloves or similar during the experiment.

Depending on class size, students can be divided into pairs or in small groups and share the tasks during this activity.

 Activity 3 Electric vehicles—viable or not?

In this activity students will investigate three different types of internet resources (blog post, commentary from an environmental organization and a news article). Which viewpoint should they believe?

You should first discuss with students that not all information found on the Internet is credible or can be trusted (has been evaluated for quality and accuracy).

A good introductory activity is to have the class brainstorm what makes a good Internet resource. If the three suggested web links are not available, it is important that students do not just search online for "electric vehicles" but look at articles that represent different viewpoints on whether the use of electric vehicles is a benefit to the environment when compared to the use of vehicles with internal combustion engines.

Remind students that there is no specific right or wrong conclusion and encourage them to formulate their own conclusion on the viability of electric vehicles.

> **INTERDISCIPLINARY LINKS**
> This activity links with the thinking critically objective of MYP Individuals and Societies in which students discuss and evaluate different sources of data and recognize their value and limitations.

 Activity 4 Monitoring the effects of acid deposition

In this activity students will design an investigation to collect and interpret data to determine the effect of acid deposition on marble statues.

There are many different variables here, including but not limited to: prevailing weather patterns, amount of annual precipitation, proximity to industrial areas, location of marble statue, etc. Many of these variables would not be applicable in a school laboratory situation. Instead students could plan to investigate the effect of temperature of the laboratory space or pH of the acid. They should control the mass and surface area of the marble sample and the volume of acid.

Students should suggest collecting at least five data points for the independent variable and repeating the experiment three times in order to collect sufficient relevant data. The length of time that students will need to wait to observe a noticeable result will depend on their design; however, it could be as little as a few days or as long as a few weeks.

> **DP LINKS**
> This activity links with Topic 8.5 in DP chemistry, in which students write the chemical equations associated with acid deposition and its reactions with reactive metals and carbonates. They also examine different methods of reducing the production of sulfur oxides.

[SAFETY]

If the activity extends to practical work, students should wear eye protection and avoid skin contact with the sulfuric acid.

TOPIC 2

Effect of increased greenhouse gases on global temperature

During this topic, students will be exposed to an area of chemistry that they will have seen on TV, read about on Internet news sites and heard their friends and family talk about. These immediate connections to an area of chemistry that is more readily accessible should allow them to bring in some prior knowledge. However, this prior knowledge may include misconceptions such as that chemistry has only negative consequences on the environment and that everything on the Internet is true. It is important that you concentrate on the science related to environmental chemistry but also allow students to be exposed to different viewpoints.

In this topic, students will investigate human causes of climate change, centred on learning about the greenhouse effect. Students will investigate what greenhouse gases are, and how their concentration in the atmosphere has increased over the past 200 years. Students will study the consequences of an increased greenhouse effect on the climate.

The consequences of greenhouse gases can be reduced, and students will consolidate their understanding of climate change, its causes and effects by reflecting on ways that climate change can be reduced.

QUICK THINK

Students should research solar cycles and long-term climate cycles caused by orbital variations (Milankovitch cycles) and understand how global warming depends on other factors as well as greenhouse gases.

QUICK THINK

Students should consolidate their understanding of Archimedes' principle: just like an ice cube melting in a glass of water, the melting of sea ice does not lead to a rise in sea level.

It is a common misconception among students that warmer oceans and poles increase the melting of glaciers and ice, which causes a rise in sea level. However, about half of the increase in sea level is due to the expansion of water as it heats up.

Furthermore, the melting of glaciers naturally occurs in summer but is historically balanced by snowfall in winter from evaporated seawater. As the climate warms, there is greater summer melting that is not balanced by snowfall as the winters are now shorter. Since there is less snowfall, there is an increase in sea level. It is the melting of ice sheets covering Greenland and Antarctica that will contribute most to the forecast sea-level rise from melting of land-based ice.

QUICK THINK

There is a broad consensus that storms are increasing in strength, or severity, due to increased sea surface temperatures, which increases "convective available potential energy".

Students could also research the effect of the jet stream. In the northern hemisphere, there is a high-altitude, high-speed stream of air called the jet stream that separates cold Arctic air from warm southern air. This river of air moves rapidly from west to east, and the greater the difference in temperature between the cold Arctic air and warm southern air, the faster and straighter the jet stream. The increase in Arctic average temperature causes a large amount of sea ice to be lost. The warmer weather also changes the shape and speed of the jet stream. The lack of cold polar air causes the jet stream to meander slowly like a river, bringing cold air further south, and warm air further north. This leads to increasing extreme weather events all over the world, such as heavy rainfall, flooding and an increase in cyclones and hurricanes.

 Activity 5 | **Greenhouse effect in a beaker**

In this activity students will investigate if carbon dioxide causes an increase in temperature inside a closed beaker.

Stage 1 of the unit planner

Key concept	Related concept(s)	Global context
Relationships	Consequences Models	Globalization and sustainability
Statement of inquiry		
Modelling the consequences of relationships can help predict global change.		

The purpose of this activity is to demonstrate to students how an increase in a greenhouse gas concentration can affect the temperature of the closed system. Students should be able, from this investigation, to fully understand the consequences of an enhanced greenhouse effect due to rising carbon dioxide levels.

Before students start this activity, they should understand what is meant by the greenhouse effect, and how the greenhouse gases affect the Earth's temperature.

During Part B students should wear eye protection.

In Part B you should explain that the reaction of vinegar and baking soda gives off carbon dioxide. Students should relate this equation to neutralization of acids and bases.

Further exploration

Students could take this investigation further by designing a lab investigation that would reduce the level of carbon dioxide in a closed system (linking this investigation to how plants use carbon dioxide during photosynthesis). Students could then write an action plan for how to reduce the carbon dioxide concentration in the atmosphere: they should focus on reducing deforestation.

Assessment

If you choose to assess students on this task, you can use criterion C. The task-specific descriptor in the top band (7–8) should read that students are able to:

- correctly collect, organize, transform and present recordings of time and changes in temperature in numerical form and correctly plot lines of best fit
- accurately interpret data and explain how the temperature changes over time in this investigation, using correct scientific reasoning
- evaluate the validity of the hypothesis based on how the presence of carbon dioxide affects the temperature of the closed system
- evaluate the validity of the method based on the conditions of the experiment, fair testing procedure and whether enough data was collected to address the question
- explain improvements or extensions to the method that would benefit investigating whether the presence of carbon dioxide in a closed system affects the system's temperature.

TEACHING IDEA 2

When teaching students about the greenhouse effect the following idea may help students further understand how the *enhanced* greenhouse effect works. Students could simulate the greenhouse effect with a box and panes of glass. Heat will be trapped in the box and the temperature inside will increase. In the atmosphere, the heat is not "trapped", but the enhanced greenhouse effect means that there are more greenhouse gases absorbing heat and emitting this back to Earth. Students could take this investigation further by investigating the relationship between temperature and the number of panes of glass or how clouds (water vapour) can affect the temperature of a closed system.

 Activity 6 **Interpreting recent data on atmospheric carbon dioxide levels**

Before students start this activity, you should discuss the fact that changes in the level of greenhouse gases occur naturally due to the carbon cycle.

Encourage students to work in groups to discuss and evaluate the graphs. Students should understand from the graphs that the level of carbon dioxide fluctuates from season to season, but overall the levels are increasing with time. The consequence of an increase in carbon dioxide levels is global warming.

Students should discuss seasonal processes that affect atmospheric carbon dioxide levels: mainly photosynthesis and respiration but also decay of organic matter. In summer months, plants use more carbon dioxide when rates of photosynthesis are higher due to increased light levels and higher temperatures; deciduous trees also come into leaf and start photosynthesizing. Respiration occurs all the time. As a result, photosynthesis increases relative to respiration during late spring and summer, and atmospheric carbon dioxide levels decrease. In winter, decay of dead plants and fallen leaves releases carbon dioxide to the atmosphere. The carbon cycle helps to maintain a balanced level of carbon dioxide in the Earth's atmosphere. However, extra CO_2 is being added to the atmosphere faster than natural processes can remove it.

This activity could be completed for homework where students must present their group findings in the next class.

Students should complete Activity 6 before starting Activity 7.

WEB LINKS

For more data on CO_2 concentration in the atmosphere at Mauna Loa, Hawaii visit:
http://cdiac.esd.ornl.gov/ftp/trends/co2/maunaloa.co2

Activity 7

Interpreting the change in carbon dioxide in the atmosphere over the past 200 years

This activity looks at the effect human activities have had on the atmospheric concentration of carbon dioxide and other greenhouse gases since the start of the industrial age.

Students could also discuss how an increase in population has affected the levels of carbon dioxide in the past 200 years.

Answers

a) Around 14 ppm (from 283 to 297).
b) Around 80 ppm.
c) Using the above values for answers to questions a) and b), around 31%.
d) Methane: around 172 ppb from 1800 to 1900, around 880 from 1900 to 2000; around 140%
    Nitrous oxide: around 15 ppb from 1800 to 1900, around 38 ppb from 1900 to 2000; around 20%.
e) The trend lines on graph A get steeper, showing the rate of change of atmospheric greenhouse gas concentration is increasing over time. The rate of increase is different for each gas: greater for carbon dioxide and methane than for nitrous oxide. In graph B, the decadal averages of the growth rate are also increasing.
f) The concentration of greenhouse gases in the atmosphere in 2030 will be significantly higher than it currently is. This is because the rate of change is not constant, but increasing. A simple prediction (linear extrapolation) is not valid. So the rise from 2010 to 2030 will be much greater than from eg 1980 to 2000, or from 1990 to 2010.
g) As the concentration of carbon dioxide in the atmosphere increases, the surface temperature of the Earth also increases. Students should use data from the simulation to justify this.

WEB LINKS

For more world population data visit:
http://en.wikipedia.org/wiki/World_population

WEB LINKS

The EPA website has useful information and activities that look at the history of climate change research and offers student activities to assess the impact of climate change on the natural environment, such as the use of tree rings to measure past climate. Teachers can use this as an introduction to the history of climate change and its measurement. Go to: http://epa.gov/climatechange/kids/ select "Educator Resources".

TIP

Students could discuss the complexities of climate change after watching or reading news articles focusing on extreme weather events in the past 10 years and how they may be attributed to a rise in greenhouse gases in the atmosphere.

QUICK THINK

Students should research the effects of global warming to date and use scientific reasoning to predict how global warming will affect the Earth in the future. They could investigate the consequences of global warming on the Earth's oceans and how these changes will impact the Arctic and the people living there.

The report "A Changing Environment – Snow, Water, Ice and Permafrost in the Arctic" from the Arctic Monitoring and Assessment Programme could be useful to students investigating the effects of global warming on the Arctic. It can be found at:

www.amap.no/

Chapter 10 | Consequences **73**

TEACHING IDEA 3

Watch Al Gore's documentary *An Inconvenient Truth* in class (or have students watch the documentary for homework). Students should answer the following questions:

1) When was the first picture of Earth, called "Earthrise", taken? (24 December 1968)

2) Name a warm cycle in Earth's climate that occurred in the last 1,000 years. (Medieval Warming Period)

3) Discuss the relationship between atmospheric CO_2 and air temperatures. (As CO_2 levels increase, the air temperature increases proportionally.)

4) By what percentage has the Arctic sea ice decreased over the past 40 years according to Al Gore? (40%)

5) We have the capabilities to reduce greenhouse gas emission levels to what they were before 1970. State as many reasons as you can for why we are not using these methods to reduce GHG emissions. (Too costly, not practical, seek more effective solution, do not recognize the severity of the issue, no political will, may not solve problem, hoping for an alternative solution.)

6) What is leading to the "collision between civilization and the natural Earth?" (Increase in the Earth's population, which is causing an increase in the consumption of natural resources. The current opinion towards the Earth and the environment. World modernization. A lack of feasible alternative energy resources.)

Summary

In the context of the impact of human activity on the environment, students have investigated consequences throughout this chapter. Students will now be able to identify consequences from observation of natural phenomena as well as from direct experimentation. By modelling interactions, students can predict the consequences of interactions and therefore also create solutions to the resulting problems.

The consequences of human activity on the environment are extensive and of extreme significance at both local and global levels. Students should be able to evaluate the impact of these consequences on the lives of themselves, their society and the global population. When integrated with their knowledge from Individuals and Societies, students should be able to develop well-evidenced arguments for solutions to the consequences of human activity.

WEB LINKS

The Biozone site contains links to news and information articles discussing the causes and effects of global warming: www.biozone.co.uk/biolinks/human-impact/

	ATL skills	Science skills
TOPIC 1 Linking form to function		
Activity 1 Comparing forearm bone structure in humans and chimpanzees	✓ Access information to be informed and inform others.	✓ Organize and present data in tables ready for processing. ✓ Interpret data and explain results using scientific reasoning. ✓ Formulate a testable hypothesis and explain it using scientific reasoning.
Activity 2 Predicting bone form in birds and mammals	✓ Make guesses, ask "what if" questions and generate testable hypotheses.	✓ Formulate a testable hypothesis and explain it using scientific reasoning. ✓ Design a method for testing a hypothesis, and explain how data will be collected.
Activity 3 Comparing the structure of different feathers	✓ Gather and organize relevant information to formulate an argument.	✓ Interpret data and explain results using scientific reasoning.
Activity 4 The surface area of shade leaves versus sun-exposed leaves	✓ Gather and organize relevant information to formulate an argument.	✓ Design a method for testing a hypothesis, and explain how data will be collected. ✓ Interpret data and explain results using scientific reasoning.
Activity 5 Variations in the number of spines on defensive leaves	✓ Make guesses, ask "what if" questions and generate testable hypotheses.	✓ Formulate a testable hypothesis and explain it using scientific reasoning. ✓ Design a method for testing a hypothesis, and explain how data will be collected.
TOPIC 2 Structure of organic molecules		
Activity 6 Naming organic compounds—a jigsaw approach	✓ Use and interpret a range of discipline-specific terms and symbols.	✓ Use appropriate scientific conventions to visually represent molecules and name organic compounds.
Activity 7 Investigating a homologous series	✓ Access information to be informed and inform others.	✓ Plot scatter graphs to identify relationships between variables.

Activity 8 Research and development of a polymer	✓ Encourage others to contribute.	✓ Design a method for testing a hypothesis, and explain how data will be collected.

Activity 9 Energy changes in a pendulum	✓ Draw reasonable conclusions and generalizations.	✓ Organize and present data in tables ready for processing. ✓ Describe improvements to a method, to reduce sources of error, and possible extensions to the method for further inquiry.
Activity 10 Investigating a factor affecting pendulum swing	✓ Use brainstorming and visual diagrams to generate new ideas and inquiries.	✓ Formulate a testable hypothesis and explain it using scientific reasoning. ✓ Organize and present data in tables ready for processing. ✓ Describe improvements to a method, to reduce sources of error, and possible extensions to the method for further inquiry. ✓ Draw conclusions, and explain these using scientific reasoning.

Introducing form

Form describes the observable features of an object or component of a system. Classifying and organizing these features provides insight into the relationship between form and function. By identifying patterns of form, students can further their understanding of structure, and predict the function that results from specific forms (and vice versa). As a result, they can use known forms to solve problems as well as synthesize new forms to provide novel functions. In this chapter, students will investigate a variety of different forms across the sciences, identifying patterns and using these to predict the associated functions.

CHAPTER LINKS
This chapter is most closely linked to Chapter 13 on function. It is also linked to Chapter 14 on patterns.

TOPIC 1 Linking form to function

In this topic, students study patterns of form in living organisms and how form is related to function. They will investigate the ratios of the length of different bones in human and chimpanzee forelimbs by collecting data and comparing this to their predictions. They will also predict what will be the differences in the densities of bird and mammal leg bones and research the function of different feather types.

Students will develop their skills in forming testable hypotheses, extracting information from a database, conducting research, collecting and analysing quantitative and qualitative data and drawing conclusions.

Activity 1 Comparing forearm bone structure in humans and chimpanzees

The forearm has a weight-supporting role in chimpanzees that is absent in humans. This kind of weight support is important in knuckle walking. The human forearm is also not adapted for hanging loads such as suspending the body from trees.

A source of information on this topic (albeit one that is academic and a challenge to interpret) is *An Introduction to Human Evolutionary Anatomy* edited by Leslie Aiello and Christopher Dean, and published by Academic Press, 1990. It is available to read online through Google Books.

	Predicted humerus to ulna length	Example humerus length (cm)	Example ulna length (cm)	Humeroulnar ratio
Human	higher	42	25	1.68
Chimpanzee	lower	27	24	1.13

Further exploration

Other ratios can be studied, such as the following.

- Humerofemoral index: ratio of humerus length to femur length.
- Brachial index: ratio of radius length to humerus length.
- Crural index: ratio of tibia length to femur length.

The bicep is attached further from the pivot point (the elbow) in chimpanzees compared to humans, increasing mechanical advantage. Students can model the human and chimp forearms using metre sticks and then quantify the mechanical advantage.

> **⊂⊃ WEB LINKS**
> To explore the argument that differences in brain structure determine differences in forearm function between humans and chimpanzees, go to:
> www.sciencedaily.com/releases/2009/03/090330200829.htm
>
> To look at the argument that structural similarities between the orangutan and the human provide support for the position that relatedness is more than gene sequence similarity, go to:
> http://news.nationalgeographic.com/news/2009/06/090623-humans-chimps-related.html

 Activity 2 Predicting bone form in birds and mammals

In this activity students will develop and test a hypothesis about whether analogous bones in different organisms have the same density.

Stage 1 of the unit planner

Key concept	Related concept(s)	Global context
Systems	Form Function	Scientific and technical innovation
Statement of inquiry		
Knowledge of the system within which a bone is found allows for prediction about its function and in turn predictions about its density.		

The local butcher's shop might serve as a source of bones (from a chicken, rabbit, cow or pig). The bones should be the same: either the femur or the tibia.

Assessment

This activity can be used to assess criteria B and C. The task-specific descriptor in the top band (7–8) should read that students are able to:

Criterion B:

- explain a problem or question to be tested by a scientific investigation such as why and in what ways bone density is expected to vary across species
- formulate and explain a testable hypothesis using correct scientific reasoning for how and why bird bone density might differ from mammal bone density
- explain how to manipulate the variables, including the precise method for consistently gathering volume and mass data, and explain how sufficient, relevant data will be collected
- design a logical, complete and safe method in which appropriate materials and equipment are selected and extraneous variables will be controlled for.

Criterion C:

- present mass and volume data as well as calculated values of density (transformed data)
- accurately interpret density values and explain results using scientific reasoning
- evaluate the validity of their hypothesis based on the outcome of the scientific investigation
- evaluate the validity of the method
- explain improvements or extensions to the method.

⌘ WEB LINKS

Bird bones on average are not necessarily less dense than other species, though it does depend on the bone. See, for example, Figure 4 in the paper *Bone density and the lightweight skeletons of birds* at : http://rspb.royalsocietypublishing.org/content/early/2010/03/13/rspb.2010.0117 The data indicates that the density of bones varies between taxonomic groups but also varies within a taxonomic group.

Some bones in the bird have air spaces in them that contribute to a bird's ventilation system, to move air through the lungs efficiently.

👤 Activity 3 — Comparing the structure of different feathers

This useful activity provides students with practice at using a strategy to organize their answers.
The table below compares flight, tail and semiplume feathers. Students may have chosen different feather types to compare.

Flight feathers	Tail feathers	Semiplume feathers
relatively long: similar length to tail feathers	relatively long: similar length to flight feathers	relatively short
no gaps between barbules	no gaps between barbules	gaps between barbules
one-sided	balanced left and right	balanced left and right

👥 Activity 4 — The surface area of shade leaves versus sun-exposed leaves

In this activity students will choose a hypothesis to test, and then design an investigation to test it.

[SAFETY]

Students should avoid nettles and other harmful leaves. They should wash their hands after the activity.

In general, shade leaves have a larger mean surface area than sun-exposed leaves of the same plant. This is an adaptation for capturing scarce sunlight.
Here is an example of how a data table can be laid out. Rather than determining surface area in this case, the longest length and greatest width were determined.

	Sun-exposed leaves		Shade leaves	
Leaf number	Length (cm)	Width (cm)	Length (cm)	Width (cm)
1	1.9	2.1	2.8	3.1
2	1.8	2.4	2.7	3.6
3	2.0	2.1	2.9	3.5
Mean	1.9	2.2	2.8	3.4

TIP

Software such as Vernier's Logger Pro can be used to determine the surface area of a leaf from a photograph.

 Activity 5 **Variations in the number of spines on defensive leaves**

This activity helps students understand that the form of a plant leaf is affected by its environment. A reasonable hypothesis is that the more difficult a leaf is for a predator to access, the lower the number of spines it has. Thus, inner leaves should have fewer spines than outer leaves and leaves higher up on the plant should have fewer spines than those lower down.

Students should consider what represents an adequate sample size. They can be provided with an exemplar graph showing a running mean for the prickliness against number of samples.

The *School Science Review* number 320, published March 2006, contains the article: "Some prickly thoughts: Does holly become more prickly when it's grazed?" This study details how this experiment can be carried out. It suggests that prickliness is not just a measure of the number of spines, but also whether the spines are all within the same plane. It found no change in the mean value being measured when the number of leaves increased beyond eight, and no significant change beyond six.

 **WEB LINKS**

The *School Science Review* number 320 can be found at: www.ase.org.uk.
Search for "school science review number 320".

Teacher instructions are available at: www.saps.plantsci.cam.ac.uk.
Search for "why does holly have prickles".

TOPIC 2   Structure of organic molecules

This topic enables students to develop an awareness and understanding of the role that organic chemistry plays in life. Organic chemistry is largely based on the chemistry of carbon and hydrogen atoms, but these two atoms do bond with a few other atoms to create millions and millions of different molecules, each with a unique form. Organic chemistry is a very large and important field of study.

Students will focus on the related concept of form as they look at basic organic nomenclature, the properties of a homologous series, and the process of making polymers. Through activities, students will develop the skills of group work and consensus, classifying and naming simple organic molecules, using an online database to gather data and investigating how to optimize the properties of a polymer by systematically varying the method.

Students will expand their knowledge of chemical nomenclature. There are some similarities with naming of covalent compounds, so you should ensure that students refer back to Chapter 9 on interaction and review their knowledge of covalent bonding. Students should also know how to use a balance or scale and how to measure amounts of substances using a variety of apparatus. They also need to be familiar with exponents and graphing negative and positive numbers on the same graph.

Activity 6   Naming organic compounds—a jigsaw approach

Students work together in a base group to develop rules for naming of branched alkanes. They then use a jigsaw approach (as explained in the student book) to form new groups and look at alkenes, alcohols and carboxylic acids. At the end of this activity they come back to their original group and teach the other members the naming rule for the organic form that they were assigned.

Structure	Name
$CH_3{-}\overset{\overset{CH_3}{\mid}}{CH}{-}CH_2{-}CH_2{-}CH_3$	2-methylpentane
$CH_3{-}\overset{\overset{CH_3}{\mid}}{CH}{-}\underset{\underset{CH_2{-}CH_3}{\mid}}{CH}{-}CH_3$	2,3-dimethylhexane
$CH_3{-}\overset{\overset{CH_3}{\mid}}{\underset{\mid}{CH_2}}{-}CH_2{-}CH_2{-}CH_3$ where the branch CH_3-CH	3-methylhexane
$CH_3{-}\overset{\overset{CH_3}{\mid}}{\underset{\underset{CH_3}{\mid}}{C}}{-}CH_2{-}CH_2{-}CH_3$	2,2-dimethylpentane
$CH_3{-}CH{-}\overset{\overset{CH_3}{\mid}}{\underset{\underset{CH_3}{\mid}}{CH}}{-}CH_2{-}CH_3$	2,3-dimethylpentane
$CH_3{-}CH_2{-}\overset{\overset{CH_3}{\mid}}{\underset{\underset{CH_3}{\mid}}{C}}{-}CH_2{-}CH_3$	3,3-dimethylpentane
$CH_3{-}\overset{\overset{CH_3}{\mid}}{CH}{-}CH_2{-}CH_2{-}CH_2{-}CH_3$	2-methylhexane
$CH_3{-}CH_2{-}\overset{\overset{CH_3}{\mid}}{\underset{\underset{CH_2}{\mid}... }{CH}}{-}CH_2{-}CH_3$	3-ethylpentane

Naming alkanes: answers

The rules for naming branched alkanes that students should come up with include:

1. Determine the longest continuous chain of carbon atoms in the molecule. This becomes the base name.

2. The carbons on the longest continuous chain are numbered so that any branches (**substituents**) that occur are located at the lowest possible number.

3. The branched chain is called the **alkyl group** and is given the same name as the corresponding alkane but the -ane ending is replaced with an -yl ending. For example, a branched -CH_3 chain attached to a C on the parent chain is named methyl.

4. a) The position of each branched group is indicated by the number corresponding to its location on the chain.

   b) If more than one of the same branched group is present, indicate that by using the Greek prefixes (di, tri, tetra, etc). The numbers are separated by commas.

   c) If two different branched groups are present, they are written in alphabetical order (the prefixes don't count for the alphabetical order). The numbers and names are separated from each other by hyphens.

The rules for naming alkenes are the same as for alkanes plus:

- The position of the C=C double bond is indicated by the number of the carbon atom where the double bond starts.
- The double bond carbons are given the lowest possible numbers (they take priority over the substituent branches).

The rules for naming alcohols are the same as naming branched alkanes, except:

- The alcohol group is named by replacing the "e" in the alkane name with "ol" and the location of the -OH group is given the lowest possible number.
- The longest chain of carbons must contain the carbon with the -OH attached.
- The number of -OH groups is indicated using the di, tri, etc prefixes.

The rules for naming carboxylic acids are the same as naming branched alkanes, except:

- The "e" in the alkane name is replaced by "oic acid".
- The number of -OOH groups is indicated using the di, tri, etc prefixes.

Structure	Name
	3-ethyl-2,3-dimethylhexane
	3-methyl-2-pentene
	4-methylhexanoic acid
	2-methyl-2-butanol
	2-methyl-1-pentene
	2,3-dimethyloctane

Structure	Name	
CH₃—CH—OH with CH₃ branch	2-propanol	
CH₃—C—C—C—OH with CH₃, H branches	2-methylbutanoic acid	**DP LINKS** This activity links with Topics 10 and 20 in DP chemistry, where students will investigate additional functional groups with respect to nomenclature, structure, reactions and reaction mechanisms.
OH—C—C—C—C with CH₃, CH₂, CH₃ branches	2-ethyl-3-methyl-1-butanol	

Naming practice of different forms of organic compounds: answers

Activity 7 — Investigating a homologous series

This activity allows students to become familiar with ChemSpider, a common chemistry database. They will use this database to investigate trends in a homologous series.

You will need to discuss with students which set of data to use when there is more than one source for the data. Students should use the Oxford University data provided on Chemspider for melting and boiling points when available, otherwise use the Alfa Aesar data. You will also need to discuss with students how to deal with data when a range of data is given.

Students will need to design their own data table and their table(s) may not look exactly the same as this one.

 **WEB LINKS**
If students need assistance with plotting multiple lines on one graph in a spreadsheet, you can instruct them to watch a YouTube video on how to do this at www.youtube.com

Alkane		methane	ethane	propane	butane	pentane
	melting point (°C)	−182	−172	−188	−138	−130
	boiling point (°C)	−164	−89	−44	−1	36
	solubility in water (mg/l)	2610	938.6	368.9	135.6	49.76
Alkene			ethene	propene	1-butene	1-pentene
	melting point (°C)	No alkene	−169	−185	−185	−165
	boiling point (°C)	No alkene	−104	−47.7	−6.3	30
	solubility in water (mg/l)	No alkene	3449	1162	354.8	210

Alcohol			methanol	ethanol	1-propanol	1-butanol	1-pentanol
	melting point (°C)		−98	−144	−127	−89	−78
	boiling point (°C)		64.7	78	97	117	136–138
	solubility in water (mg/l)		1×10^6	7.921×10^5	2.715×10^5	7.67×10^4	2.089×10^4
Carboxylic acid			methanoic acid	ethanoic acid	propanoic acid	butanoic acid	pentanoic acid
	melting point (°C)		7–9	16.7	−20.8	−5	−34
	boiling point (°C)		100–101	118.1	140–141	164	184–186
	solubility in water (mg/l)		9.553×10^5	4.759×10^5	1.736×10^5	6.606×10^4	1.86×10^4

Homologous series data for alkanes, alkenes, alcohols and carboxylic acids with 1-5 carbons.

 DP LINKS

This activity links with DP chemistry Topic 10 in which students will examine and explain trends in a homologous series for a larger number of functional groups.

 Activity 8 **Research and development of a polymer**

Students are most likely to have already met organic molecules in the form of polymers. Polymers exist in both natural and synthetic forms.

In this activity, students attempt to create a polymer bouncing ball that has the highest bounce when dropped from the height of 1 metre. Students can use a metre stick and drop the balls from the top of the stick, taking the mean of three bounce heights.

The properties of the polymer can be altered by changing the method and procedure. This activity goes beyond just trial and error as students are limited in how many variations of the composition of the ball they can make, as they have a budget of 7.50 chembits with which to test and develop this polymer form. The procedure, and the optimal amounts that students should conclude, are:

1) Add 10 cm³ of white glue to a small beaker.

2) Add 2.5 g of borax to 5 cm³ of water and stir.

3) Add the borax solution to the white glue and stir.

However, students can also get a good bouncing ball without these exact amounts.

[SAFETY]

Students should wear eye protection, and avoid skin contact with the borax and glue. They should wear disposable gloves when moulding and testing the bouncing balls. They should not take the balls out of the laboratory.

This activity is best done in small groups so that students can discuss the procedure and trial process.

TEACHING IDEA 1

To continue investigating the different polymer forms of organic molecules, students can bring in different samples of plastic containers that are labelled with resin identification codes (this could be a triangle with a number and code such as 1 PETE). Remove the codes from the objects and have students work in a group to identify the plastics based on a series of simple tests (water test: float or sink / copper wire test: flame colour / alcohol test: float or sink / acetone test: reaction or no reaction / oil test: sink or float / heat test).

Complete details for this activity, including a flow chart to aid identification of the plastics from the test results, can be found at: www.monroecounty.gov/Image/plastics_analysis_lab_lesson.pdf

Students should appreciate that many types of plastic are available with very different properties, according to the form of the monomer and its side chains. The tests show that different polymers can be sorted by density.

TOPIC 3   Forms of energy

Students will extend their knowledge of energy by focusing on the forms it takes. They will also look at the way energy changes its form during energy transformations. The activities are focused on understanding how energy is conserved as it changes from one form to another. The activities focus on gravitational potential and kinetic forms of energy. Students will use their mathematical skills to investigate the relationship between these two forms of energy. They will discover why, in the absence of friction, a pendulum can continuously swing.

The students will also discuss if energy is infinite or not, and look at where it comes from. This links to Chapter 5 on energy, which discusses fusion in the Sun as our ultimate source of energy on Earth.

Activity 9   Energy changes in a pendulum

This activity is extremely useful for students to see the conservation of energy. It also encourages students to use their mathematical skills to prove a law.

It is very important that students are aware of what the terms "gravitational potential" and "kinetic energy" refer to. They should be familiar with manipulating both formulae. A good way to introduce this topic is to show the video in the web links to the students. Then have a discussion about how a swing works.

Emphasize to students that the string needs to be as long as possible and, provided the angle is small, they can try greater heights above the starting position.

Students should discuss the difference between the actual and theoretical velocity. The difference can be due to any of the following: human error (in starting and stopping the stopwatch), not dropping the weight from the same height on each trial, parallax in action, air resistance that is not taken into account in the theoretical value, the pivot point not offering a smooth swing or creating a lot of friction, or the pendulum shape not being aerodynamic.

Suggested improvements can include ensuring that parallax is not a problem by being at eye level with the pendulum, using a heavier weight with a streamlined shape (which will be less affected by air resistance), testing the pivot point and making it as smooth as possible, or using a pulley system if necessary. Students can measure the velocity directly with a light gate and data logger.

Further exploration

Students can research how pendulums are used in buildings at:
http://phys.org/news/2013-08-japanese-companies-quake-damping-pendulums.html

> **TEACHING IDEA 2**
>
> For students who are struggling with the concept of the conservation of energy between kinetic and potential energy, visit the skate park animation at http://phet.colorado.edu/en/simulation/energy-skate-park
>
> The site also has many worksheets to accompany the animation that will help develop students' understanding of this concept.

 Activity 10 Investigating a factor affecting pendulum swing

In this activity students will design an experiment to investigate one factor affecting the time of a pendulum swing and will apply the knowledge they have discovered in Activity 9.

It is important that the students carry out Activity 9 before Activity 10 as it is essential to their understanding. Students can use the set-up from Activity 9 with their improvements. They will have a good understanding of the mathematical approach required for the assessed activity.

Stage 1 of the unit planner

Key concept	Related concept(s)	Global context
Form	Energy Change	Scientific and technical innovation
Statement of inquiry		
Energy changes from one form to another.		

> **TIP**
>
> If the students are struggling with the pendulum concept, refer them to the swing video mentioned earlier. It will relate the "swinging" to real life.

In preparation for this activity, the class can develop a mind map to discover the most appropriate dependent and independent variables. As a class, they can discuss how to develop and improve their procedure (including the set-up of the pendulum) from the mistakes that they observed in Activity 9.

If students are struggling with an independent variable to choose for their investigation, tell them to use a mind map. Then discuss this with them and ask them which of their factors will give the best results, prompting them to look at mass or the height that the pendulum is dropped from. The dependent variable is the time of the pendulum swing, and they should control length of string and either mass or height of pendulum depending on which is the independent variable.

[SAFETY]

If the pendulums are constructed by weight, ensure that the students are aware of the danger of standing too close as it is swinging. Check all set-ups before the students begin to record results.

Assessment

If you choose to assess students on this task, you can use criterion B or C. The task-specific descriptor in the top band (7–8) should read that students are able to:

Criterion B:

- formulate a testable hypothesis based on their knowledge of the pendulum and correctly explain it using scientific reasoning
- explain how to manipulate and control the variables, and explain how data will be collected with a clear results table.

Criterion C:

- present collected and transformed data; they should also show examples of any processed data that they have in their results tables
- accurately interpret data and explain results using the formulae for potential and kinetic energy
- evaluate the validity of their hypothesis based on the outcome of their investigation
- evaluate the validity of the method (did they learn how to reduce sources of error and give more accurate results to improve the experiment from Activity 9?).

TEACHING IDEA 3

To extend students, ask them to research how potential and kinetic energy are used to engineer roller coasters. The students can design their own roller coaster and use the formula to work out the speed at each of the points along the track and present it to the class.

⊂⊃ WEB LINKS

This link will help students carry out the roller coaster investigation in Teaching idea 3:
www.teachengineering.org/view_lesson.php?url=collection/cub_/lessons/cub_energy/cub_energy_lesson01.xml

This link can aid students' basic understanding of energy:
www.bbc.co.uk/schools/gcsebitesize/science/add_aqa/kinetic_energy/kineticact.shtml

Summary

In all three sciences, it is often possible to understand function by observing form. In each of the activities in this chapter, students have studied patterns of form and how the functions of various objects change as a consequence of their form. Students should be able to design experiments to investigate how form affects function and gather sufficient data to identify patterns and create models. Students have learned how the integration of knowledge about form and function can lead to the development of objects with novel properties and unique functions. The study of form facilitates the study of function. Thus, this chapter is ideal preparation for the activities in Chapter 13 on function.

CHAPTER 12 Movement

	ATL skills	Science skills
TOPIC 1 Movement in plants and animals		
Activity 1 Kinesis—investigating woodlice motion in response to a stimulus	✓ Apply existing knowledge to generate new ideas, products or processes.	✓ Formulate a testable hypothesis and explain it using scientific reasoning. ✓ Design a method for testing a hypothesis, explaining how to manipulate the variables and how enough data will be collected. ✓ Organize and present data in tables ready for processing. ✓ Interpret data gained from scientific investigations and explain the results using scientific reasoning.
Activity 2 Kinesis—analysis of data of motion in response to a food source	✓ Interpret data.	✓ Design a method for testing a hypothesis, explaining how to manipulate the variables and how enough data will be collected. ✓ Interpret data gained from scientific investigations and explain the results using scientific reasoning.
Activity 3 Investigating thigmotropism in the sensitive plant	✓ Select and use technology effectively and productively.	✓ Design a method for testing a hypothesis, explaining how to manipulate the variables and how enough data will be collected.
Activity 4 Analysing data related to seed dispersal	✓ Interpret data.	✓ Interpret data gained from scientific investigations and explain the results using scientific reasoning.
TOPIC 2 Electrochemistry and movement of electrons		
Activity 5 Activity series of metals	✓ Draw reasonable conclusions and generalizations.	✓ Interpret data gained from scientific investigations and explain the results using scientific reasoning.
Activity 6 Creating the best voltaic cell	✓ Collect and analyse data to identify solutions and make informed decisions.	✓ Interpret data gained from scientific investigations and explain the results using scientific reasoning.

Activity 7 Investigating forces	✓ Process data and report results.	✓ Formulate a testable hypothesis and explain it using scientific reasoning.
		✓ Organize and present data in tables ready for processing.
		✓ Plot scatter graphs with a line of best fit and identify trends.
		✓ Describe improvements to a method, to reduce sources of error.
Activity 8 Measuring velocity	✓ Gather and organize relevant information to formulate an argument.	✓ Formulate a testable hypothesis and explain it using scientific reasoning.
		✓ Organize and present data in tables ready for processing.
		✓ Plot scatter graphs with a line of best fit and identify trends.
		✓ Describe improvements to a method, to reduce sources of error.
Activity 9 Measuring acceleration	✓ Analyse complex concepts and projects into their constituent parts and synthesize them to create new understanding.	✓ Organize and present data in tables ready for processing.
		✓ Calculate the gradient of a straight-line graph.
		✓ Interpret data gained from scientific investigations and explain the results using scientific reasoning.
		✓ Plot scatter graphs with a line of best fit and identify trends.
		✓ Describe improvements to a method, to reduce sources of error.

Introducing movement

Movement refers to the change in position of a substance. This movement can range in scale from the movement of an electron to that of a planet. While some objects that move are easily observable (a train), the movement of others such as ions or electrons can only be measured indirectly by investigating their interactions and relationships with other measurable variables. This chapter focuses on the theoretical science (explaining why movement occurs) and on the important question of how we measure movement.

The activities in this chapter help students design experiments that enable the collection of data to determine factors that influence movement, and measure the extent to which movement has occurred. The concept of movement has excellent links with the key concept of

TIP

To introduce the idea of movement, ask students to brainstorm as many types of movement as they can. Ask them to highlight both the largest and smallest things that move. Retain this list until the end of the unit.

relationships, because movement can be determined by the link between two or more components of a system. Once the relationships have been established, students can use them to predict the movement of the components in different situations.

TOPIC 1 # Movement in plants and animals

In this topic, students will investigate movement of animals and plants in response to a stimulus or stimuli. They will investigate the motion of woodlice using a choice chamber, investigate thigmotropism in the sensitive plant, analyse data related to seed dispersal and investigate some of the variables that affect flight distance of winged seeds.

Students will develop their skills in formulating a hypothesis and designing a procedure to test it; controlling variables; analysing data, evaluating the method and drawing conclusions.

Activity 1 — Kinesis—investigating woodlice motion in response to a stimulus

This activity allows students the experience of forming hypotheses and testing them through experimentation. It also provides students with experience in devising novel experiments as well as experience with the ethical treatment of animals in the context of the laboratory setting.

[SAFETY]

If students collect woodlice and handle them, they should wash their hands after doing so.

Ten woodlice should be introduced into a choice chamber that has half of its area covered and half open to the light. After 30 minutes, the number of woodlice found in each half of the chamber should be counted. This should be repeated over five more half-hour intervals.

WEB LINKS

The webpage entitled "Using a choice chamber to investigate animal responses" can provide teachers with some helpful hints for scaffolding this practical in the classroom. It can be found on the Nuffield Foundation Practical Biology site: www.nuffieldfoundation.org/practical-biology

DP LINKS

Section A4 of the DP biology course explores invertebrate behaviour that promotes survival.

Sample answer table

	30 minutes	60 minutes	90 minutes	120 minutes	150 minutes
Dark	6	8	10	9	6
Light	4	2	0	1	4

Activity 2 Kinesis—analysis of data of motion in response to a food source

Answers

a) (i) 1,450 m (±20) m
   (ii) 980 m (±20) m
b) Shark 2 turns / changes direction more often than shark 1.
c) Shark 1 swims in water where the zooplankton levels are low.
   Shark 2 swims in water where the zooplankton levels are higher.
   Shark 2 turns more often because it is feeding in food-rich water and shows the highest degree of turns where zooplankton levels are highest.
   Shark 1 turns less often because it is still searching for food and there is not much to eat.
d) Among possible reasons are: water temperature, other sharks / competitors, mates, water currents, pollution.

Further exploration

Databases and websites exist that allow students to follow whale movements. For example, the National Geographic education website has a "mapping blue whale migration" activity at http://education.nationalgeographic.com/.

 **DP LINKS**

Activities 2 and 4 in this chapter are useful for offering students experience with the style of questions they will find in the DP biology exams.

 Activity 3 Investigating thigmotropism in the sensitive plant

In this activity students will design an investigation to measure the effect of one of the aspects of thigmotropism.

When touched, the leaves along one stalk of a *Mimosa* plant will close instantly. They take approximately 10 minutes to re-open.

TIP

Mimosa plants can be grown from seeds obtained through online suppliers. There are a number of plant species other than *Mimosa pudica* that visibly display the "sensitive" response. These include catclaw mimosa (*Mimosa pigra*), the Venus flytrap (*Dionaea muscipula*), wild sensitive pea (*Cassia nictitans*) and bladderwort (*Utricularia purpurascens*).

WEB LINKS

The *Plants-in-Motion* website provides time-lapse videos of a range of plant motions. They can be found at: http://plantsinmotion.bio.indiana.edu/plantmotion/starthere.html

 Activity 4 Analysing data related to seed dispersal

In this activity the students answer questions on seed dispersal.

Answers

a) Height 0.54 m: 60–79 cm / 0.60–0.79 m (from the plant); height 10.8 m: 0–299 cm / 0–2.99 m (from the plant).
b) The greater the height from which the seed fell, the further it travelled from the parent plant.
c) *At the greater height:* seeds can catch the wind to travel farther / updrafts carry seeds farther / there is more wind at greater heights; when the seed is dropped farther from the ground it does not travel straight down / there is more time for the seeds to be blown before hitting the ground.
   At lower height: seeds can fall straight down; seeds can hit downdraft and fall faster.

TOPIC 2 — Electrochemistry and movement of electrons

This topic will enable students to explain the role that the movement of electrons has in redox reactions. Students will probably not be aware of the frequency with which redox reactions appear in their lives. Some of the many common everyday examples of redox reactions are: corrosion (rusting); photochromic glass lenses (in spectacles that automatically darken in the sunlight); combustion of fuels; nitrogen fixation in fertilizers; photosynthesis; metabolism; bleaching agents; and black-and-white print photography.

Students will focus on the related concept of movement as they discover how the movement of electrons can explain redox reactions. They will develop an activity series of metals, and construct a voltaic cell to produce the maximum voltage. Through these activities, students will develop the skills of using a computer simulation to gather data, and designing a procedure to investigate the effect of an identified variable on the voltage produced by a voltaic cell.

TEACHING IDEA 1

At the end of the topic, you can ask students, in groups, to research one of these everyday occurrences and relate it to what they have learned. The final outcome of this research would be a PowerPoint presentation or Prezi that students would present to their class.

 Activity 5 — Activity series of metals

Using an online simulation to perform a series of reactions between metals and salt solutions will allow students to perform many different reactions in a safe environment and gather repeat data.

In order for students to make the most accurate conclusions, ensure that they collect observations on all the possible reactions.

The list of metals that students should obtain, in order from most reactive to least reactive, is Mg, Zn, Fe, Ni, Sn, Pb, (H), Cu and Ag.

Possible answers

- If a metal is reactive, its metal ion is not very reactive.
- Information in an activity series allows chemists to predict the outcome of a chemical reaction; allows chemists to predict reactions of metals with acids; and helps to predict how to extract metals from their ores.
- Some metals only occur as ores (their salt form) as they are very reactive. Other metals occur naturally in the environment as they are not very reactive.
- Metals that only occur as salts must be extracted from their salt using a reduction reaction. This reaction could be using a more reactive metal to displace the metal from a solution of its salt. For example, copper can be extracted from a copper sulfate solution by placing a more reactive metal such as iron into the solution. Another example is the thermite reaction, in which iron can be extracted from iron (II) oxide by heating it with aluminium, which is more reactive. Another type of reduction reaction is electrolysis. By electrolysing the molten salt, metal ions gain electrons to form metal atoms.

Further exploration

For each reaction they observe, students can write the half-reactions. For those combinations that had no reaction, students should indicate that no reaction has taken place.

 DP LINKS

This activity links with Topic 9 in DP chemistry, where students will deduce the feasibility of a redox reaction from information in a more extensive activity series.

QUICK THINK

A salt bridge is necessary to maintain electrical neutrality; it acts to supply positive and negative ions to both half-cells so that the overall charge remains neutral.

Activity 6 Creating the best voltaic cell

Activity 6 will allow students to apply the information they gained in Activity 5 to investigate the variables that affect the voltage produced by a given cell.

You should provide students with a copy of a more extensive activity series corresponding to the available metal electrodes. You will find a more detailed activity series, one that expands on the one that students developed in Activity 6, in the DP chemistry data booklet, which is available to IB World Schools on the Online Curriculum Center (OCC).

The outcome of this activity will be determined by the possible electrodes that students will be able to use. These will be limited to the electrodes that you have available in the laboratory. Common electrodes for student use include Fe, Cu, Sn, Mg, Zn and Ni. You need to ensure that you have corresponding salts for students to make electrolytic solutions. A rolled-up piece of filter paper soaked in a solution of potassium nitrate or sodium chloride can be used to construct a salt bridge.

[SAFETY]

Students should wear eye protection and avoid skin contact with the copper and zinc sulfate solutions.

There are several variables that students can investigate in this activity, for example: concentration of electrolytic solution; composition of the salt bridge; mass of the electrode; dimensions of the electrode; identity of the electrodes; and identity of the electrolyte.

WEB LINKS
To find an online activity series, search "activity series" at http://chemistry.about.com/

DP LINKS
This activity links with Topic 9 in DP chemistry in which students will study two different types of electrochemical cell—voltaic and electrolytic.

TEACHING IDEA 2

Ask students to research different types of batteries (cells) and then create something visual (poster, blog, webpage, series of photos, etc) that represents their research. An accompanying written report should include, but is not limited to, the following questions:

- What role does the movement of electrons play in this battery?
- How does your research relate to the information covered in this chapter and topic?
- What are the half-reactions involved?
- What is the maximum voltage produced by this type of battery?
- What are the uses of this battery?
- What are the benefits of this type of battery over other batteries?
- What are the disadvantages of this type of battery over other batteries?

The different types of battery that students could research include, but should not be limited to:

- Nickel-cadmium battery
- Nickel metal hydride battery
- Lithium ion battery
- Dry cell/alkaline battery
- Sealed lead-acid battery
- Zinc-air battery
- Lithium cells
- Fuel cells
- Lithium polymer battery
- Nickel/sodium cells
- Carbon-zinc battery

Velocity and acceleration

Activities in this topic are focused on mechanical movement. They allow students to practically investigate factors that affect motion in terms of displacement, time, velocity and acceleration. The purpose of these activities is to get students thinking critically of the relationships between variables in mechanical motion.

For this topic, students will discuss the difference between velocity and acceleration. They will focus on force as a vector and what balanced and unbalanced forces are.

CHAPTER LINKS
This topic links well with Chapter 15 on environment, where gravity is discussed in the context of the warping of space—time.

TEACHING IDEA 3

If students are finding the motion graphs difficult to interpret, you can set up several different demonstrations of movements in the class for students to watch, for example: a basketball being tossed into a net, plastic bowling pins, a video of a roller coaster ride, a video of a skateboarder in a half pipe. In groups, students must explain each of the situations in terms of displacement, velocity and acceleration. Students should be prompted to note the idea of positive and negative motion and draw qualitative motion graphs of their observations.

QUICK THINK

To find the velocity and acceleration of athletes at different stages of the 100-metre race, students can use the equation:

$$\text{acceleration} = \text{change in velocity/change in time}$$

and the data at:

http://speedendurance.com/2008/08/22/usain-bolt-100m-10-meter-splits-and-speed-endurance/

Students can use their calculated accelerations for each 10-metre interval to discuss the notion that sprinters have a large acceleration at the start of the race, but as they reach their top velocity, there is a smaller change in velocity; therefore, the sprinter's acceleration decreases during the race.

Students can also compare the velocities of a 200-metre sprinter to that of a 100-metre sprinter, and calculate and compare the acceleration of a sprinter in a 100-metre and 200-metre race for similar intervals.

QUICK THINK

When the parachutist jumps, his or her weight is greater than air resistance so he or she accelerates. The downward force (gravity) is greater than the upward force of air resistance.

When the parachute opens, the upward force of air resistance on the parachute increases. The resultant downwards force decreases and, therefore, the speed of the parachutist decreases.

WEB LINKS

For a video that explains speed and velocity go to:
www.teachertube.com
and search for "rchs physics podcast 2.1 speed
and velocity".

Activity 7   Investigating forces

Before this activity students need to have an understanding of what balanced and unbalanced forces are. They will also need to understand that for balanced forces, the resultant force is zero. Unbalanced forces have a resultant force equal to the difference between the forces acting on an object. Students will just be looking at the force they exert on the ring compared to the force exerted by their partner. When the ring does not move, the values of the two forces are equal, and the resultant force is zero. When the forces are varied, the student pulling with the greatest force will find that the metal ring moves towards them. In this case, the resultant force is the difference in the two force measurements. The Newton meters (spring scales) should have a range of 10 N.

Discussion answers

a) Examples of balanced forces:

- A person standing on the floor: the floor pushes up on the person and the force of gravity pulls them down.
- Hanging objects such as a picture on a wall: the weight of the object pulls it down while the tension in the cord pulls up.
- A boat: the weight of the boat on the water is balanced by the upthrust from the water.

Examples of unbalanced forces:

- A truck accelerating in a given direction.
- A roller coaster when the cars are accelerating.
- When two people push against each other with one person overpowering the other.

b) When a car driver suddenly applies the brakes, the driving force from the engine becomes less than the resistive forces (from the brakes and from friction between the tyres and the road) and there is a resulting force in the opposite direction to the direction of motion. This causes the car to slow down.

Further exploration

Ask students to use three strings attached to three Newton meters and adjust the pulling forces until the ring is in static equilibrium. They should note the reading on each force meter and also measure the angles between the strings, using a protractor to mark the direction of the forces on a diagram. Discuss with the students the fact that the resultant of any two of the forces is equal and opposite to the third force.

TEACHING IDEA 4

To continue the discussion of balanced and unbalanced forces, examine the case of the descent of a parachutist before and after opening the parachute. Ask students to identify the forces and predict the shape of the velocity–time graph. Explain the meaning of terminal velocity.

Students could also investigate whether terminal velocity can be reached for a model parachute dropped down a stairwell.

Activity 8 — Measuring velocity

In this activity students will investigate how changing the angle of the ramp changes the average velocity of a toy car as it rolls down the ramp.

Stage 1 of the unit planner

Key concept	Related concept(s)	Global context
Relationships	Movement Function	Science and technical innovation
Statement of inquiry		
Relationships in movement have important functions in technical innovation.		

Before this activity, students need to have an understanding of what is meant by average velocity. Students should understand the variables that affect velocity (displacement changes with time). Students should be able to calculate velocity when given the displacement of an object and the time taken.

[SAFETY]

If heavy wooden ramps are used, they should be placed where they will not easily fall off benches or tables. Placing the ramps on the floor or on a large bench is best. Do not place ramps between two tables. If wooden trolleys are used, place something for catching the trolley at the bottom of the ramp. Crumpled paper or polystyrene beads in a cardboard box will suffice as a buffer.

As an alternative to finding average velocity as described in the student book, students can use ticker tape apparatus. Light gates can be used to find the velocity at a fixed point near the bottom of the ramp. Students should be shown how to set up and use light gates/ticker tape correctly. They should practise finding the velocity of an object using ticker tape by attaching the tape to the object. Move the object a distance x. Count the number of dots on the ticker tape. A ticker tape timer takes 0.1 seconds to make 5 dots. Students can find the average velocity of the object by dividing the distance travelled (length of the tape) by the time.

WEB LINKS
There is an excellent resource for understanding how to use a ticker tape apparatus at www.physicsclassroom.com Search for "ticker tape diagrams".

Students should understand that for the method described in the student book and for the ticker tape method, they are calculating the car's average velocity over the whole ramp.

Students should predict that an increase in the angle of the ramp will increase the average velocity of the car. This is because at greater angles to the horizontal, less horizontal force is opposing the car; therefore, the resultant downward force acting on the car increases and the car moves faster. The car travels the same distance in less time.

The independent variable is the angle of ramp (degrees), the dependent variable is velocity (m/s). Controlled variables are the mass of the car and the length and type of surface.

If protractors are not available, students can determine the angle of incline of the slope by using the following formula:

$$\theta = \tan^{-1}(\text{height/base})$$

Conclusion and evaluation answers

a) Students should find from their graph that as the angle of ramp increases, the velocity of the car increases.

b) The hypothesis is supported if the results followed an expected trend and there were very few anomalies in the data.

INTERDISCIPLINARY LINKS
In MYP mathematics, students study algebra and trigonometry. These techniques can be used to collect their data in Activities 9 and 10.

c) Possible sources of error include: angle of ramp was not measured correctly; controlled variables were not kept constant; the car did not travel in a straight line; human error using the stopwatch (though the size of this error is reduced by finding the mean of three trials as described in the method and having a different person use the stopwatch each time, because each person has a different reaction time and will stop the stopwatch at slightly different times); friction between the car and surface, though this should be constant for each ramp angle unless there are imperfections on the ramp (bumps/holes, etc).

d) Possible improvements include: use an air track to remove friction between the car and the surface it moves on (or use a smooth ramp); perform more trials and average the results; use a light gate to reduce timing errors (if light gates were not used).

e) To extend the investigation, students can change the surface the car travels on. For a smoother surface, the average velocity is greater at the same ramp angle and using the same car.

Assessment

If you choose to assess students on this task, you can use criterion C. The task-specific descriptor in the top band (7–8) should read that students are able to:

- correctly collect data, organize, transform and present data for angle versus velocity in numerical form and as a scatter graph with line of best fit
- accurately interpret data and explain what effect a change in ramp angle has on the average velocity of an object moving down the ramp
- evaluate the validity of the hypothesis based on the outcome of how the angle affects the velocity
- evaluate the validity of the method based on the conditions of the experiment, fair testing procedure and whether enough data was collected to address the question
- explain improvements that would increase accuracy by minimizing the effect of errors and explain extensions to the method that would benefit the scientific investigation, by investigating the effect of a different variable.

 Activity 9 **Measuring acceleration**

In this activity students will investigate the change in acceleration as the angle of a ramp changes.

Before starting this activity you should ensure that your students understand the relationship between velocity and acceleration. Using what they have learned in Activity 8, students should be able to predict that there is a change in velocity as the ball rolls down the slope. This will result in the ball accelerating as it goes down the slope.

Key concept	Related concept(s)	Global context
Relationships	Movement Function	Science and technical innovation
Statement of inquiry		
Scientific innovations can occur through understanding the relationships between functions of movement.		

Before starting this experiment, students should have performed all steps in Activity 8 as the conceptual understanding is similar for both.

[SAFETY]

If heavy wooden ramps are used, they should be placed where they will not easily fall off benches or tables. Placing the ramps on the floor or on a large bench is best. Do not place the ramps between two tables. Place something for catching the trolley at the bottom of the ramp. Crumpled paper or polystyrene beads in a cardboard box will suffice as a buffer.

Students should predict that the greater the slope of the incline, the larger the acceleration of an object down the incline. This is because the force of gravity is causing the object to accelerate down the ramp. However, the full force of gravity is not acting on the object because gravity is opposed by the ramp. The steeper the ramp, the greater the force of gravity acting on the object; therefore, the greater the acceleration of the object.

The independent variable is the angle of incline; the dependent variable is the object's acceleration. Controlled factors are:

- Mass of object. The same object will be rolled down the slope each time.
- Length/surface of track. The same track will be used each time.
- Time of trial. The motion sensor will record the object's movements for the entire length of the track (start to finish)/ or ticker tape is used.

If protractors are not available, students can determine the angle of incline of the slope by using the following formula:

$$\theta = \tan^{-1}(\text{height/base})$$

The tape chart produced is in the shape of a speed–time graph. The steps on the tape charts should be of equal size (the increase in speed is the same for each strip), showing that the acceleration is constant. As an extension to the method described in the student book (which finds only the change of speed between the first and last sections), students can plot a speed–time graph for several segments of their tape chart and calculate the gradient of the line of best fit.

Conclusion and evaluation answers

a) Based on the data collected in this investigation, students should find that a larger angle of incline results in a higher rate of acceleration for an object travelling down the incline.

b) The hypothesis is supported if the results followed an expected trend and there were very few anomalies in the data.

c) Possible sources of error include height/angle of ramp were not measured correctly; controlled variables were not kept constant; or object did not travel in a straight line.

d) Possible improvements include: reduce friction between the object and surface it moves on; perform more trials and average the results; use light gates at the top and bottom of the ramp to measure the instantaneous speeds; and automatically measure the time interval between the light gates.

Further exploration

Discuss with students that the total distance travelled by the object is the full length of the tape, and explain the total area beneath a speed–time graph represents the total distance travelled.

Students can further their understanding of acceleration by investigating other factors that affect motion such as how the mass of an object affects its acceleration, and how friction affects motion. In principle, the mass of the object is irrelevant because in a frictionless situation, it will have an acceleration equal to g down the slope. However, friction reduces the acceleration and the effect is greater for an object with a small mass.

Assessment

If you choose to assess students on this task, you can use criterion C. The task-specific descriptor in the top band (7–8) should read that students are able to:

- correctly collect data, organize, transform and present data for ramp angle versus acceleration in numerical form and as a scatter graph with line of best fit
- accurately interpret data and explain what effect a change in angle has on the acceleration of an object
- evaluate the validity of a hypothesis based on the outcome of how the angle affects the acceleration
- evaluate the validity of the method based on the conditions of the experiment, fair testing procedure and whether enough data was collected to address the question
- explain improvements that would benefit the scientific investigation, by reducing the effect of measurement errors.

DP LINKS

In DP physics Topic 2, students will determine instantaneous and average values for velocity, speed and acceleration. They will also study:

- solving problems using equations of motion for uniform acceleration
- sketching and interpreting motion graphs
- determining the acceleration of free-fall experimentally
- analysing projectile motion, including the resolution of vertical and horizontal components of acceleration, velocity and displacement.

QUICK THINK

The student should understand that when a car hits something, it will decelerate quickly. An accelerometer detects this change in speed. If a large enough deceleration is detected (compared to deceleration from normal braking) the airbag circuit is triggered. A current is passed through a heating element. This ignites an explosive gas and nitrogen is given off in the reaction. The gas inflates a nylon bag as the nitrogen expands. As the driver moves forward against the airbag, this causes the gas to dissipate through small holes in the edges of the bag. All this takes place within 30–40 milliseconds after the crash. The bag reduces the deceleration of the car's occupant so that it is less than that of the car itself. By reducing the person's deceleration, the force with which they collide with the interior of the car is reduced, and the chance of injury reduced.

TIP

If students struggle to understand deceleration and airbags, have them discuss their experiences of being a passenger in a car. Ask them to describe how you know you are accelerating or decelerating in a car. Use their answers to discuss inertia in moving cars.

 **WEB LINKS**

Students can use the following link to learn how to design an airbag. Go to:
www.sciencenetlinks.com
and search "it's a crash test dummy".

TEACHING IDEA 5

Show students the following videos regarding airbags and discuss what features of an airbag makes it effective:

www.youtube.com/watch?v=d7iYZPp2zYY&feature=related

www.youtube.com/watch?v=A2fAgW_1nD0&feature=related

www.youtube.com/watch?v=2eCPa9wz2xI

www.physorg.com/news/2011-10-motors-center-mounted-airbags-video.html

Note: The mathematics behind this is too difficult for the majority of MYP students. Students can be given a table to fill in while they watch the videos. Students should write down their observations of what happens with an airbag and what happens without an airbag. Students must explain their observations using scientific reasoning.

🏃 TAKE ACTION

Students have learned about velocity and acceleration. They have applied their understanding to airbags and car safety. They can take their ideas further by investigating how to make our roads safer. Students can research braking distance and factors that affect the braking distance. They can then promote safe driving by raising awareness by speaking in school assemblies, or putting up posters in school.

Ask students to repeat the introductory exercise. Once completed, compare this to the first attempt to reflect on what they have learned about the scale of the types of movement.

Summary

Movement can be assessed on many different levels. By understanding the causes of movement at each level, students can model processes and the movement of the constituent components. Throughout this chapter, the activities have focused on how we quantify and measure movement. At each level of analysis and within each science, there are different techniques that can be employed to manipulate and measure movement, and students should now be aware of the strengths and limitations of these. After creating models and observing movements in experiments, students can integrate their knowledge about interactions to make predictions about movements.

Function

	ATL skills	Science skills
TOPIC 1 Function in organisms		
Activity 1 Two-point discrimination	✓ Recognize unstated assumptions and bias.	✓ Formulate a testable hypothesis using scientific reasoning. ✓ Design a method to test a hypothesis, and select appropriate materials and equipment. ✓ Ensure sampling is random to avoid selection bias. ✓ Interpret data gained from scientific investigations and explain the results using scientific reasoning.
Activity 2 Motor neurons and mirror drawing	✓ Test generalizations and conclusions.	✓ Design a method to test a hypothesis, and select appropriate materials and equipment.
Activity 3 The function of fruit colour	✓ Apply skills and knowledge in unfamiliar situations.	✓ Design a method to test a hypothesis, and select appropriate materials and equipment.
TOPIC 2 Function of acids and bases		
Activity 4 Identification of substances	✓ Test generalizations and conclusions.	✓ Interpret data gained from scientific investigations and explain the results using scientific reasoning.
Activity 5 Neutralization	✓ Interpret data.	✓ Interpret data gained from scientific investigations and explain the results using scientific reasoning.
Activity 6 Which antacid is the most effective?	✓ Collect and analyse data to identify solutions and make informed decisions.	✓ Design a method to test a hypothesis, and select appropriate materials and equipment. ✓ Interpret data gained from scientific investigations and explain the results using scientific reasoning. ✓ Describe improvements to a method, to reduce sources of error.
Activity 7 Buffering capacity	✓ Gather and organize relevant information to formulate an argument.	✓ Design a method to test a hypothesis, and select appropriate materials and equipment.

Activity 8 Making a pinhole camera	✓ Revise understanding based on new information and evidence.	✓ Interpret data gained from scientific investigations and explain the results using scientific reasoning. ✓ Use appropriate scientific conventions to visually represent refraction. ✓ Use appropriate scientific terminology to make the meaning of your findings clear.
Activity 9 Refraction of light through different media	✓ Make guesses, ask "what if" questions and generate testable hypotheses.	✓ Interpret data gained from scientific investigations and explain the results using scientific reasoning. ✓ Create accurate, labelled scientific drawings.
Activity 10 Investigating a factor affecting the refraction of light	✓ Apply existing knowledge to generate new ideas, products or processes.	✓ Formulate a testable hypothesis using scientific reasoning. ✓ Design a method to test a hypothesis, and select appropriate materials and equipment.

Introducing function

Function describes the role, purpose or behaviour that is being measured in any given experiment. In this chapter, students will study the function of different systems and their constituent parts and measure how these change as variables are manipulated. This concept is excellent for teaching all three key concepts together and demonstrates the interconnectivity between and within the key concepts and the different areas of science.

As the students progress through the activities, they learn how to measure particular functions, and how to apply this knowledge in real-world situations to help solve problems. It is important to highlight the differences between human applications of function and the natural underlying phenomena. This also exemplifies how scientific understanding of the world enables us to influence change.

TOPIC 1 Function in organisms

In this topic, students further investigate how form is related to function, by looking at the function of the nervous system and colour in fruit. They will investigate two-point discrimination ability, mirror drawing and the processing of visual information and how environmental conditions affect colour changes in ripening fruit.

Students will develop their skills of designing an experiment, forming and testing a hypothesis, conducting research and collecting, recording and organizing data.

TIP

Find interesting examples whereby something has two distinct functions and ask the students to identify the function. Although this could require some research, it is excellent for highlighting how function is context-dependent within a system. Here are some examples:

- Provide students with sodium bicarbonate and ask them for its functions in baking and cleaning.
- Provide them with yeast and ask about its functions in brewing and baking.
- Provide them with a magnet and ask about its functions in compasses and televisions.

Activity 1 Two-point discrimination

This activity looks at why sensory neurons in different parts of the body have different receptive field areas, and goes on to design an experiment to investigate whether two-point discrimination is fixed or whether it can be influenced by external variables.

Differences in two-point discrimination on different parts of the body are due to differences in the receptive field of a single neuron. If the receptive field is small, then it is likely that the two points fall within two receptive fields. In the fingertip, the distance between nerves is small so the points are touching different receptive fields. In the shoulder, the distance between nerves is greater so the two points are touching the same receptive field.

Two-point discrimination, like all acts of perception, can be tricked. Distraction has an impact. Expectation has an impact. If the skin is cold, then the ability to differentiate is reduced.

There is variation between different people when measuring the discrimination in the same body area. If the skin has callouses, then discrimination will be reduced. Age and injury also influence nerve function.

Since the procedure is relatively easy to carry out, carrying out at least three repeats per distance, per area is advised.

The question of how large a difference is significant is an opportunity to introduce the concept of statistical testing.

 Activity 2 Motor neurons and mirror drawing

The success of mirror drawing can be influenced by a number of factors such as the complexity of the image, and task learning or repetition. Learning by increasing the number of attempts taken (up to, say, 15) can reduce the time taken, while the number of points in the figure increases the time taken. These are both quantitative variables that can be analysed using a line graph. Innate factors also have an effect; students will differ significantly in their hand–eye coordination and spatial visualization. Age can also have an effect. Ask students to examine whether left-handers perform better at mirror drawing.

The hardboard sheet ensures students cannot directly view either the star or their hand when making their drawing. Students can only view the object and their hand through a mirror that reverses the image. Adjust the height of the hardboard sheet accordingly. Students should start tracing from the same point each time.

Further exploration

Students can also explore cross-education (whether improved skill in one hand is achieved following practice with the other hand).

 Activity 3 The function of fruit colour

This activity looks at fruit ripeness, colour and the function of fruit pigments in ripe and unripe fruit.

Fruits have features designed to enhance dispersal by organisms such as birds, primates and other fruit-eating animals. The bright colour of many fruits evolved to attract dispersal agents. Colour is a visible indicator of maturity and ripeness.

Colour is not the only property that changes as a fruit ripens. There are changes in the carbohydrate composition that result in sugar accumulation and increased sweetness. There are changes in texture and in the firmness of the flesh of fruits as well as changes to the chemicals produced and accumulated.

Note: Red, green and blue (RGB) values are a function of the device that is doing the reading. This means it is not straightforward to compare RGB values measured using different devices. There are also factors such as illumination conditions (light source colour, intensity and direction; object reflectivity/absorbance) to consider. However, this method is less subjective than visual estimation using a colour chart. To classify the fruit into underripe, ripe and overripe categories, students can obtain a range of mean RGB values for each fruit type and desired ripeness category.

Temperature can have an impact on ripening. Cold can either slow ripening or accelerate it. The presence of other ripening fruit can also have an impact on the ripening process. For example, placing unripe fruit into a bag with other ripe fruit and sealing the bag can accelerate the ripening process.

WEB LINKS

Plants in action is an online textbook that has a section on fruit ripening that goes into some detail about the ripening process. It can be found at:

http://plantsinaction.science.uq.edu.au/

Scientific American also has an article that outlines the origin of fruit ripening at:

www.scientificamerican.com/article/origin-of-fruit-ripening/

TOPIC 2 | Function of acids and bases

In this topic, students will focus on the related concept of function by looking at the functions of acids and bases, and what role indicators have in their function. Students will devise a scheme for classifying different substances; perform a neutralization reaction and observe the function of an indicator; design a procedure to identify the most effective antacid; and design a study to determine whether acid precipitation will affect fish farm stocks.

Students will have heard of some common acids such as hydrochloric acid, citric acid and sulfuric acid. They will also have heard of some common bases such as sodium hydroxide and ammonia.

TEACHING IDEA 1

Ask students to examine the labels of household goods for the names of acids and bases and to make a list of them. Once students have generated the list, they can research the function of each substance. For example, is the substance a flavour enhancer, a preservative or a surfactant? The final outcome will be a collaborative class list of common acids and bases and their functions.

Before students examine more closely the phenomenon of function in relation to acid/base chemistry, they should be (re)introduced to microscale techniques and review their knowledge of collecting accurate data and control variables.

In this activity students will examine three main ways to classify and identify solutions: using indicators; using a conductivity meter; and using the reaction between a metal and a solution. The concentration to use for both the test and reagent solutions is 0.1 M. For the conductivity test, you can use either a conductivity meter or a simple circuit with a battery and 1.5 V bulb.

The following table shows what students should observe.

		Test solutions (0.1 M)						
		HCl	NaOH	H_2SO_4	HNO_3	KOH	$Ba(OH)_2$	H_2O
Test reagents	Phenolphthalein	colourless	pink	colourless	colourless	pink	pink	colourless
	Bromothymol blue	yellow	blue	yellow	yellow	blue	blue	yellow
	Universal indicator	red	purple-blue	red	red	purple-blue	purple-blue	green
	Magnesium	bubbles form; gas released	should not be any reaction	bubbles form; gas released	bubbles form; gas released	should not be any reaction	should not be any reaction	no reaction
	Calcium nitrate	no visible reaction	a small amount of white precipitate may form	a small amount of white precipitate may form	no visible reaction	a small amount of white precipitate may form	a small amount of white precipitate may form	no visible reaction
	Conductivity	conductor	conductor	conductor	conductor	conductor	conductor	non-conductor
	Litmus paper	red	blue	red	red	blue	blue	no change

Based on these observations, students should be able to list generalizations that will help them identify the unknown solutions.

Among the general properties for acids, bases and salts, students should make the following observations:

- Blue litmus paper turns red in an acidic solution and red litmus paper turns blue in a basic solution.
- Phenolphthalein is colourless in acid solution and pink in a basic solution.
- Bromothymol is yellow in an acid solution and blue in a basic solution.
- Universal indicator is red in an acid solution and purple-blue in a basic solution. Acids are red when mixed with universal indicator while bases are purple-blue.
- Acids react with magnesium to form small bubbles while basic solutions have no reaction.
- Calcium nitrate solution is not useful in identifying unknown solutions.
- Ionic solutions will conduct electricty while molecular compounds are not conductors.

DP LINKS

This activity links with DP chemistry Topic 8 where students will further investigate the properties of acids and bases, and further examine the function of indicators.

Students should identify the mystery substances based on the following observations.

	Test solutions (0.1 M)							
	$(NH_4)_2SO_4$	C_2H_5OH	HCl	NaOH	$CaCl_2$	$Ca(OH)_2$	$HC_6H_7O_7$	$C_6H_{12}O_6$
Phenolphthalein	colourless	colourless	colourless	pink	colourless	pink	colourless	colourless
Bromothymol blue	yellow	yellow	yellow	blue	yellow	blue	yellow	yellow
Universal indicator	red	green	red	purple-blue	green	purple-blue	orange/yellow	green
Magnesium	no visible reaction	bubbles form; gas released	bubbles form; gas released	should not be any reaction	should not be any reaction	should not be any reaction	bubbles form; gas released	no visible reaction
Calcium nitrate	a small amount of white precipitate may form	no visible reaction	no visible reaction	a small amount of white precipitate may form	no visible reaction	no visible reaction	no visible reaction	no visible reaction
Conductivity	conductor	conductor	conductor	conductor	conductor	conductor	conductor	non-conductor
Litmus paper	red	no change	red	blue	no change	blue	red	no change

(Test reagents — row label for left side)

[SAFETY]

Ensure that eye protection is worn and that due care is taken when handling these chemicals.

Activity 5 — Neutralization

In this activity students will perform a neutralization reaction between hydrochloric acid and sodium hydroxide (a base).

Unlike a typical neutralization reaction using a burette, this neutralization reaction is done on a microscale. This allows students to use smaller amounts of solutions. Students should produce sodium chloride, which is a neutral salt; the litmus test they perform should confirm this. From this observation, students should conclude that mixing an acid with the "right" amount of base will result in a neutral solution. Neutralization reactions are important if there is an acid or base spill in the laboratory, or as a possible solution to acid deposition.

In order to produce the salt sodium nitrate, students would have to react nitric acid with sodium hydroxide.

DP LINKS

This activity links with DP chemistry Topic 8, in which students perform calculations involving acids and bases, and Topic 18, in which students examine neutralization using pH curves.

[SAFETY]

Ensure that eye protection is worn and that due care is taken when handling these chemicals. Ensure that, when heating the evaporating dish on the hot plate (or alternative heating source), students heat very gently and allow the liquid to evaporate slowly.

Activity 6 **Which antacid is the most effective?**

In this activity students must prove which of the samples of antacid are the most effective at neutralizing acid.

Key concept	Related concept(s)	Global context
Relationships Systems	Evidence Function Patterns	Scientific and technical innovation
Statement of inquiry		
The relationship between the function of a substance and evidence observed during reactions helps predict a substance's chemical behaviour.		

The number and types of antacids that students are able to test depend on what is locally available. The procedure that students devise could be similar to the microscale neutralization reaction performed in Activity 5 or could be a full-scale titration. Alternatively, it could be one that is completely their own design.

Students will need to perform a trial or test to see if their procedure would work with the amounts that they suggest, with the apparatus that they suggest and within the time available.

The variables that students plot will depend on their chosen procedure. Students do not have to numerically calculate the effectiveness of the antacid, just produce a ranked list of the most effective antacid to least effective antacid. When students compare their results with the other groups in the class, it will be important to discuss any discrepancies between groups.

[SAFETY]

Ensure that eye protection is worn and that due care is taken when handling these chemicals.

Activity 7 **Buffering capacity**

In this activity students will design a study to determine whether or not acid precipitation will affect the fish farm stocks.

Key concept	Related concept(s)	Global context
Relationships Systems	Evidence Function Patterns	Fairness and development
Statement of inquiry		
The relationship between how a substance functions in a chemical laboratory helps predict how a substance will function in the natural environment.		

Although this is a hypothetical situation, students can use the Internet to research a real local fish farm or even arrange a visit. Major freshwater fish that are farmed include salmon, carp, tilapia, catfish, trout, blue mussel, oyster and clam.

⚭ WEB LINKS

To help students narrow down what to search, you can instruct students to search with the keyword "aquaculture". A good website that gives information on the types of fish farmed across the globe is at: www.thefishsite.com

⚭ DP LINKS

This activity links with DP chemistry Topic 8 in which students will take a closer look at acid deposition, and the same topic in the DP environmental systems and societies course.

TOPIC 3 — Function of the eye and spectacles

In this topic, students will investigate the functions of an eye and the refraction of light though different media. There are activities in which students think critically about how scientists use information about the functions of the eye to correct people's vision.

Students will make a pinhole camera and use the properties of a pinhole camera to try to establish the functions of a human eye. The students will also complete an activity on measuring the refractive index of different media. This involves trigonometric functions so it is very important that the students have a basic understanding of *sine* in relation to mathematics.

🔗 **CHAPTER LINKS**

This topic links slightly to Chapter 7 on transformation where students learn about visible light as part of the spectrum of electromagnetic waves, and the relationship between speed, frequency and wavelength.

🔗 **DP LINKS**

This topic links with DP physics Topic 4 about oscillations and waves, specifically wave properties.

 Activity 8 — **Making a pinhole camera**

In this activity, students will compare the functions of an eye to a pinhole camera. The students will need to have studied the functions of an eye before this activity, so they are able to distinguish between the functions present in both a pinhole camera and the eye, and those that are not.

Students must record any observations that they make during the activity.

Discussion question answers

a) Each ray of light passing through each hole will create its own image, resulting in many images. The smaller the holes, the better focused the image will appear.

b) The pinhole camera works because light travels in straight lines. The image is upside down because light from the top of the object being viewed (a tree) passes through the pinhole in a straight line and through the box onto the screen. Light from the bottom of the tree also passes through the pinhole and onto the screen. However, if you draw a diagram of this you will see that the rays of light cross over and thus the image is upside down.

c) The image will be brighter because there is more light now hitting the screen. It will also be less focused because there is more light being used, and therefore it will hit a wider part of the screen. If the hole gets too big then there will be no image at all.

d) When the lens is placed in front of the hole it will focus the light rays on the screen. This makes the image more clear/focused.

e) The pinhole camera is similar to the eye as both have an image formed on a screen. When the lens is placed in front of the hole then the image becomes more focused. This is the function of the lens in the eye: making an image more and less focused. Both images are in colour. The image is brighter if more light is let in. If the hole is smaller, the image is more focused (this is why we squint when something is difficult to see).

Further exploration

Students can research why we squint when we are trying to focus on what we are seeing.

TIP

It is useful to have different diagrams available to the students showing how a pinhole camera forms an image of different light sources (a lit candle or an illuminated tree) and with more than one pinhole. This will help them understand how light travels through a pinhole camera and the effect it has on the image.

QUICK THINK

Dr Joshua Silver's invention of liquid-filled, adjustable lenses enabled manufacturers to make lenses more affordable to people in developing countries. Silicone oil is injected between two flexible membranes protected by a hard plastic layer. The adjustable shape makes it possible for people to create their own glasses to fit their needs. The syringe and tubing used to inject the gel are removed and the glasses are tightened into place.

TEACHING IDEA 2

To help students understand the idea of refraction, place a pencil in a glass of water and ask students to explain why the pencil now appears bent. This can be done before Activities 9 and 10.

Discus the hunting habits of birds in relation to hunting fish and how they take into consideration that the fish is not in the place that they see due to refraction. Here is a link to help explain this: www.bbc.co.uk/learningzone/clips/refraction/13525.html

 Activity 9 **Refraction of light through different media**

In this activity students will measure the refractive index of glass and acrylic glass.

[SAFETY]

Warn students to take care as the ray box lamp will get hot enough to burn skin. Do not use glass prisms with chipped or sharp edges.

Students should predict that the acrylic glass block will cause light to bend the most, because it has a lower refractive index, so the speed of light in that material will be slower (bigger contrast with speed of light in air). Students need to be familiar with the trigonometric function *sine* and how to calculate *sine* of various numbers on their calculator. If they do not already know this, they should be informed before the activity. Students also need to be able to use a protractor to measure angles. You should make sure that all students are measuring the angle correctly. If available, polar graph paper could help students measure the angles. If there are students who are particularly weak at the mathematics side of science, keep a careful watch on them as they will struggle with some of the calculations.

TIP

Semi-circular blocks are better to use in this experiment as you have to deal with two refractions in parallel-sided blocks—one at each interface.

WEB LINKS

The "Snell's law of refraction" video by QuantumBoffin on www.youtube.com can be shown to students to demonstrate how to set up Activity 9.

Discussion question answers

a) The different materials have refractive indexes. Light travels faster in the block with the smaller refractive index, which gives a greater angle of refraction for the same angle of incidence. The refractive index is a constant for any material, so changing the shape or thickness of the block does not change the angle of refraction at an interface.

b) If students investigated a rectangular block, they will have seen that the incident ray and refracted ray are parallel to each other (because the outgoing ray is bent away from the normal by the same amount as the incoming ray is bent towards the normal) but laterally displaced. For different thicknesses of rectangular blocks of the same material, the amount of lateral displacement of the ray changes. For a thin block, the ray is only offset by a small amount. The thicker the block, the more the ray is offset.

Further exploration

Students can investigate total internal reflection (including the critical angle).

Activity 10 | **Investigating a factor affecting the refraction of light**

In this activity students will plan their own experiment to explore the refraction of light in various media.

Key concept	Related concept(s)	Global context
Relationships	Patterns Function	Scientific and technical innovation
Statement of inquiry		
Investigating and discovering the relationship and analysing patterns in materials can help us gain a better understanding of those materials.		

The students must complete Activity 9 to be able to understand and design their experiment for this activity.

Brainstorming questions answers

a) White light travels in a straight line. It bends as it passes through a medium. White light can be dispersed (split up into constituent colours).

b) What medium the light travels through; the intensity of the light; the colour of light.

c) The medium that it travels through. The colour will also affect the refraction as the different colours have different wavelengths and therefore refract differently.

d) Refraction is the bending of light as it passes from one medium to another.

e) The medium, the intensity and the colour of the light.

Assessment

If you choose to assess students on this task, you can use criterion B or C. The task-specific descriptor in the top band (7–8) should read students are able to:

Criterion B:

- explain a question to be tested about a factor affecting the refraction of light
- formulate and explain a testable hypothesis on factors affecting refraction of light, using correct scientific reasoning about the independent variable and how it will affect the refractive index or the angle of refraction
- explain how to manipulate the variables, and explain how sufficient relevant data will be collected; for example, explaining why at least five values of the independent variable will be tested, why repeat measurements will increase confidence in the conclusion and how other factors will be controlled
- design a logical, complete and safe method in which appropriate materials and equipment are selected to investigate the factors that affect the refraction of light, including how each variable will be measured and an awareness of the hazards from the hot ray box lamp.

Criterion C:

- correctly collect, organize, transform and present data in numerical form, for example calculations of refractive index or of wavelength from frequency of light, and plot a scatter graph with a correctly drawn line of best fit
- accurately interpret data and explain results using correct scientific reasoning, for example with reference to refractive index and wavelength of light
- evaluate the validity of their hypothesis based on the outcome of their investigation
- evaluate the validity of the method based on conditions of the experiment, fair testing procedure and whether enough data was collected to address the question
- explain improvements to the method that would reduce sources of error, or extensions that would benefit investigating the factors that affect the refraction of light.

Summary

In this chapter, students have studied function in various contexts. They should now understand why certain systems function as they do and how to measure the impacts of a changing environment on them. Students should now be able to identify function as a consequence of structure and also suggest aspects of form from measured functions. Students should also appreciate that an understanding of function can be applied to advance scientific knowledge, explain processes and potentially solve problems.

Function can be viewed on a system or component level, with many interactions occurring simultaneously. Students should now be able to construct experiments to isolate interactions and negate bias and thus investigate specific functions and their consequences. The study of function should help students place their knowledge of systems, relationships and change into many different contexts, allowing for deeper understanding and synthesis of knowledge across topics.

Patterns

	ATL skills	Science skills
TOPIC 1 Classification		
Activity 1 Interpreting a dichotomous key	✓ Make inferences and draw conclusions.	✓ Interpret data gained from scientific investigations and explain the results using scientific reasoning.
Activity 2 Creating a dichotomous key of fruits	✓ Organize and depict information logically.	✓ Formulate a hypothesis using scientific reasoning. ✓ Organize and present data so that conclusions can be drawn. ✓ Create accurate, labelled scientific drawings.
Activity 3 Analysing giraffe coat patterns	✓ Build consensus.	✓ Interpret data gained from scientific investigations and explain the results using scientific reasoning.
TOPIC 2 The periodic table		
Activity 4 Examining the patterns found in the periodic table	✓ Process data and report results.	✓ Organize and present data so that conclusions can be drawn. ✓ Plot scatter graphs and identify trends on graphs. ✓ Interpret data gained from scientific investigations and explain the results using scientific reasoning.
Activity 5 Metal, non-metal or metalloid classification	✓ Collect, record and verify data.	✓ Organize and present data so that conclusions can be drawn. ✓ Interpret data gained from scientific investigations and explain the results using scientific reasoning.
Activity 6 Taking a closer look at the elements in a group	✓ Access information to be informed and inform others.	✓ Interpret data gained from scientific investigations and explain the results using scientific reasoning.

Activity 7 Electron arrangement in atoms	✓ Make connections between various sources of information.	✓ Create accurate, labelled scientific drawings. ✓ Plot scatter graphs and identify trends on graphs. ✓ Interpret data gained from scientific investigations and explain the results using scientific reasoning.
Activity 8 The island of stability	✓ Revise understanding based on new information and evidence.	✓ Make connections between scientific research and related economic factors.
TOPIC 3 Standing wave patterns		
Activity 9 Creating a variety of standing waves with 2, 3 and 4 nodes	✓ Collect, record and verify data.	✓ Make sketches of observations from an experiment.
Activity 10 Visualizing standing waves in the microwave oven	✓ Gather and organize relevant information to formulate an argument.	✓ Interpret data gained from scientific investigations and explain the results using scientific reasoning. ✓ Describe improvements to a method, to reduce sources of error.
Activity 11 Visualizing sound waves	✓ Make connections between subject groups and disciplines.	✓ Make sketches of observations from an experiment.

Introducing pattern

The identification of patterns enables us to classify and organize events, allowing us to draw conclusions and predict future consequences. By investigating the relationship between different phenomena, we are able to find underlying trends that provide a basis for testing a hypothesis or making new predictions.

Underlying patterns can be those that already exist in nature, or they can be in systems created by humans in order to help understand a problem. In this chapter, students will study a variety of patterns and classification systems. This presents excellent opportunities for inquiry into pattern identification. Students will also be able to investigate the many different ways to represent patterns within and across the sciences.

As students progress through the activities, they will attempt to identify their own patterns and systematically classify their knowledge. This process will require them to integrate knowledge across topics and thus consolidate their understanding.

TOPIC 1   Classification

In this topic, students will use patterns in the visible characteristics of plants and animals to decide if two species are related. They will interpret a dichotomous key, create a key to identify different fruits and analyse patterns in the dark patches of different subspecies of giraffe.

Students will develop their skills in classifying objects and assessing hypotheses. They should have prior knowledge of reproduction in flowering plants: pollination, fertilization and seed germination and the flower's associated structures.

 Activity 1   Interpreting a dichotomous key

In this activity students will look at a key listing a group of beetles and use the patterns listed to identify each species from the diagrams below the key.

Answers

A. Oil beetle

B. longhorn beetle

C. Colorado beetle

D. weevil

E. ladybird

 Activity 2   Creating a dichotomous key of fruits

In this activity students will construct a dichotomous key based on the features they observe in a range of fruits.

[SAFETY]

Take care with sharp knives and always cut down on a board, keeping fingers clear. Students should not taste or eat any of the fruit.

The teacher can decide how technical the terminology should be that is used to create the key. There are many possible dichotomous keys.

Example answer key

1a	Fruits occur singly	Go to 2
1b	Fruits occur in clusters of two or more	Grapes
2a	Thick skin that separates easily from flesh	Lemon; orange
2b	Thin skin that adheres to flesh	Go to 3
3a	One seed per fruit	Go to 4
3b	More than one seed per fruit	Go to 5
4a	Skin covered with velvety hairs	Peaches
4b	Skin smooth, without hairs	Plums
5a	Dry fruit	Pomegranate
5b	Wet fruit	Go to 6
6a	Containing a hard, inner layer	Pear, apple
6b	No hard, inner layer	Red pepper; tomato

If the concepts of phylogeny and shared characteristics have been addressed in class you could also ask students to deduce evolutionary relationships.

Activity 3 Analysing giraffe coat patterns

This activity looks at the coat patterns of giraffes.

Example answers

A comparison of the fur patterns of the four variants:

A. West African: The dark patches have lower percentage cover than reticulated or Masai; size of individual dark patches is greater than Rothschild or Masai but smaller than reticulated.

B. Rothschild: The patches are the most brown/least red of the four; they represent the lowest percentage cover of the four.

C. Reticulated: The patches are the largest and represent the greatest percentage cover of all the varieties.

D. Masai: The pattern is the most jagged/least regular of the four; similar percentage cover to Rothschild.

The percent age cover of different patches can be determined using a method similar to the one used to measure leaf area in Activity 4 of Chapter 11.

Variant	Habitat	Vegetation	Estimated temperature range (°C)
West African	Southwestern Niger	tiger bush; Niger delta drought resistant	31–41
Rothschild	Uganda and Kenya	savanna, woodlands, seasonal floodplains	22–32
Reticulated	Kenya, southern Ethiopia and Somalia	savanna, woodlands, seasonal floodplains	30–40
Masai	Central and southern Kenya and Tanzania	savanna, woodlands, seasonal floodplains	20–28

A testable hypothesis regarding camouflage is that if the patterns are a form of camouflage, then vegetation should vary in the habitat of different subspecies to explain variations in the coat patterns.

Using the heat regulation hypothesis, one might predict that giraffes confronted with higher habitat temperatures should have higher levels of heat exchange channels under their coats.

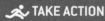 **TAKE ACTION**

Overall, the number of giraffes declined sharply in the first decade of the 21st century. One estimate suggests a 40% decline. The Rothschild giraffe is an endangered subspecies according to the IUCN. Students can be encouraged to join efforts of conservation organizations to preserve giraffe habitat. The African Wildlife Foundation and the Giraffe Conservation Foundation are two such organizations.

TOPIC 2 The periodic table

The importance of pattern permeates the study of science and chemistry is no exception. A central idea of chemistry—the periodic table—was developed from regular elemental patterns including the "hidden" patterns predicted by Mendeleev. Modern chemists are trying to extend the number of known elements based on patterns exhibited by the properties of elements in the periodic table. Teaching this topic will enable students to understand the patterns that exist in the periodic table. They will then be able to use these patterns in the study of many different areas of chemistry.

In this topic, students will focus on the related concept of pattern as an introduction of the ideas of periodicity and electron arrangement. First, students will be placed in a similar position to that of Mendeleev 150 years ago when they arrange known elements based on known properties. Students will use an online database to look for patterns in several elemental properties, then investigate patterns in the three main classes of elements: metals, non-metals and metalloids. Students will examine trends that exist in groups of elements, examine trends in electron arrangement in atoms, and finally investigate how scientists "create" new, superheavy elements.

Before students examine the concept of pattern more closely, they should review their knowledge of using a spreadsheet to record and graph data, and be able to follow simple laboratory procedure.

TEACHING IDEA 1

Ask students to research the concept of patterns in their everyday lives and then relate it to the patterns found in the periodic table. How are they similar? How are they different? Students can illustrate their research in a poster, a journal article, a blog post, song lyrics or a photo collage.

Students can also investigate other areas in chemistry where patterns exist (organic chemistry, biochemistry, polymer chemistry, etc).

 Activity 4 **Examining the patterns found in the periodic table**

Students will make use of two different online databases to investigate the relationships and trends in four properties: electronegativity, first ionization energy, atomic radius and ionic radius. Students should draw the following conclusions:

a) Electronegativity increases going across a period (left to right) and decreases going down a group/increases going up a group.

b) First ionization energy increases going across a period (left to right) and decreases going down a group/increases going up a group.

c) Atomic radius decreases going across a period (left to right) and increases going down a group/decreases going up a group.

d) Ionic radius decreases going across a period (left to right) until the metals give way to non-metals, when there is a increase in ionic radius; across the non-metals there is also a decrease in ionic radius going left to right. Ionic radius increases going down a group/decreases going up a group.

 DP LINKS

This activity links with DP chemistry Topic 3 and Topic 13, where students will be able to explain why these and other additional periodic trends occur.

Activity 5 **Metal, non-metal or metalloid classification**

In this activity students will investigate samples of unlabelled elements with respect to the properties listed in the student book.

The samples of elements that students will use depends on what samples are available in your school's laboratory storage. However, students will need samples of all three major classifications. Possible samples include: iron, carbon, magnesium, nickel, sulfur, copper and silicon. Do not label the samples with the element's identity, as students will be asked to classify these unlabelled elements as either belonging to the metals, non-metals or metalloids.

For the conductivity test, you can use either a conductivity meter or a simple circuit with a battery and 1.5 V bulb. For the reactivity with acid test, depending on the element being tested, the reaction may be very visible and immediate or may be very slow; students should be encouraged to label the test tubes used in the reactivity test and leave overnight.

 DP LINKS

This activity links with DP chemistry Topics 3 and 13. In these topics, students will predict and explain the metallic and non-metallic behaviour of an element based on its position in the periodic table, and closely examine the properties of the transition metals.

Students should record their observations in a data table.

Here is a possible format:

	Conductivity	Malleability	Appearance	Reactivity with acid
Element A				
Element B				
Element C				
Element D				
Element E				
Element F				
…				
Element Z				

[SAFETY]

Students should wear eye protection and avoid skin contact with the acid.

 Activity 6   Taking a closer look at the elements in a group

In this activity students will use an online source of information to learn about the elements and trends that exist in their families.

Give each student group a different group of the periodic table to investigate. After watching the videos for elements in the same group, students will collate the information they have seen with regard to the patterns that are seen within a group. They can comment as to what patterns are observed; does this trend increase or decrease down a group, etc. Different student groups can present their findings to the remainder of the class; then as a whole-class discussion, students should investigate the trends that exist in different groups in the periodic table.

 DP LINKS

This activity links with DP chemistry Topic 3 where students will discuss the similarities and differences in properties of elements in the same group.

QUICK THINK

Students should research one of five alternative models for the periodic table. Group students according to which alternative model they choose. Students must prepare to defend their choices in a class debate.

TEACHING IDEA 2

Students can also research, design and present an alternative periodic table.

Activity 7   Electron arrangement in atoms

In this activity students will learn to examine two ways of communicating the pattern of electrons for the first 20 elements: electron shell diagrams and electron arrangement. Students should come up with the following electron shell diagrams:

🔗 DP LINKS

This activity links with DP chemistry Topic 2 in which students will write the electron configuration for all elements in the periodic table in both long form and core notation.

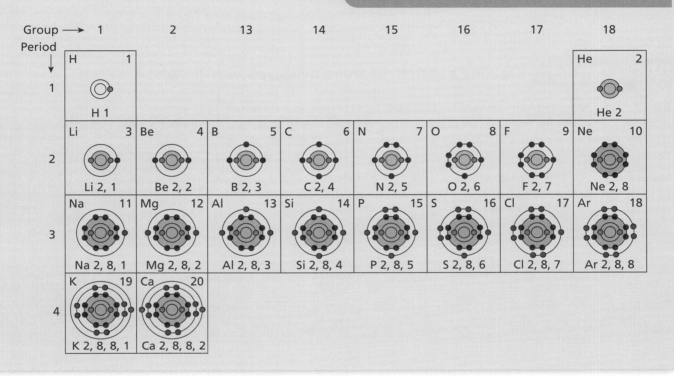

Activity 8   The island of stability

In this activity students will consider whether or not the hunt for "new" elements should continue, after looking at the process scientists go through to create a new element at the end of the periodic table.

Students can consider the two questions individually or, alternatively, they can debate the two positions as a class. Ensure students appreciate that element 114 was created based on achieving "magic numbers" of protons and neutrons in the nuclear shell model, broadly analogous to the stable electron configurations of the noble gases.

TOPIC 3   Standing wave patterns

This topic describes the patterns of waves and how these patterns have affected our instrument making. This topic links very well with Chapter 8 on models. Students will be introduced to new concepts and vocabulary (node, antinode and harmonics). They should have an understanding of each word before they do any of the activities. They will also need to be able to distinguish between constructive and destructive waves.

The activities in this chapter focus on visualizing various waves and discovering their patterns. There are links throughout the chapter to applications of these patterns in real life, including how standing waves in a microwave oven affect the cooking of food.

🔗 CHAPTER LINKS

Students must understand vocabulary from Chapter 8 on models. This includes terms such as "frequency" and "wavelength".

 **DP LINKS**
This topic links to DP physics under Topic 4 about oscillations and waves. The vocabulary learned in this chapter is used throughout this topic.

WEB LINKS
Extra information on standing waves can be found at: www.physicsclassroom.com

It also has a variety of worksheets available on this topic. Go to this website, then to "physics tutorial", then to "waves". Lesson 4 is all on standing waves.

Before Activity 9, it is useful to discuss what transverse waves are. This has been covered in Topic 3 in Chapter 8 on models.

 Activity 9 Creating a variety of standing waves with 2, 3 and 4 nodes

This activity is used to help students visualize a standing wave. It is very important that students understand what nodes and antinodes are. They also need a basic understanding of a fundamental harmonic. The fundamental harmonic consists of one antinode between two nodes.

As this activity is only based on visualizing patterns there is very little to write up. Students simply have to comment on how much force they used versus the number of nodes they observed. They should note that the more energy exerted, the more frequent the nodes.

TIP
Make sure the students are aware that they need to hold one of the ends static in order for the activity to work.

QUICK THINK

This is about destructive wave interference. This means that (if there is no turntable) no heat energy is reaching parts of the food. This can result in the food being half-cooked and the other half still raw.

 Activity 10 Visualizing standing waves in the microwave oven

This is a homework activity because not all school labs will have enough microwave ovens for the students. Students will need to have a basic understanding of how microwaves work before they can do this activity at home. This can be achieved during the lesson in a discussion activity. All the necessary information is in the student book.

It may be helpful to discuss the procedure during the lesson so students can ask questions in class. Make sure students understand that they must remove the turntable from the microwave so that the pieces of toast do not rotate. When the students bring their results in the next lesson, go through the various reasons as to why you multiply the value by two (because the distance between the melted butter is between two crests). It is a good idea to make the students take pictures of their pieces of toast at home after they have completed the experiment to prove that they carried it out. They can put the pictures in their books under the experiment.

TIP
A good alternative to buttered toast is to use a layer of mini marshmallows or chocolate buttons/chips. Note that heating for too long increases melting and you can't as easily find the point to measure from.

Discussion question answers

a) From their experiment, students should be able to determine that, because a microwave works using electromagnetic waves and the waves are constantly bouncing off the walls inside the microwave, constructive and destructive interference occurs. The result of constructive interference at antinodes and the continual movement of the food on the turntable ensures maximum mean energy is transferred and the food will be hotter. Destructive interference causes nodes where no energy is transferred so the food stays cold.

WEB LINKS
Go to: www.planet-science.com/ and search for "chocolate wavelength" for more detail on this method.

b) Students are using different microwave ovens, which may not all operate at 2.45 gigahertz. However, students should consider that they are measuring from the "centre" of the melted butter. This is not a precise instruction about where to measure from, so they might all measure from different places. Also, measurements are limited to the nearest millimetre, which is a fairly large uncertainty in comparison with the separation of the antinodes (around 6 cm). The students who get a value close to the range given in the book are the most accurate. This will link nicely to the end of the topic where students discuss random errors.

c) Students should discuss that they need a very clear understanding of what and where the "centre" of the melted butter is. They can obtain more accurate results by repeating the experiment and taking a mean of the measurements—this will take account of some of the random errors caused by the difficulty of judging where the antinodes are. They can also discuss the instruments they used and their sensitivity. For example, a ruler with a millimetre scale is better than a ruler with a centimetre scale.

Further exploration

Students can go a step further and determine the speed of light using the wavelength found from the microwave. Microwaves are a form of electromagnetic radiation and therefore travel at the speed of light. Ask students to research how wavelength, frequency and the speed of light all link up: speed of light is equal to wavelength multiplied by frequency. It is very important that students know the frequency for an average microwave. They can research this (or look on the back of the oven). Their answer should be 2.45 gigahertz. This is 2.45 billion times per second. The following is the calculation the students should make if their measured wavelength is 12.1 cm:

$$12.1 \times 2,450,000,000 = 29,645,000,000 \text{ cm/s}$$

As speed of light is expressed in m/s this must be divided by 100 to give: 296,450,000 m/s, which is pretty close to the accepted value of the speed of light: 299,792,458 m/s.

TEACHING IDEA 3

Before reading the text on accuracy and precision, students could be asked to look up the definition of these terms on various websites. They could then compare the definitions found and determine if the definitions are all the same. This could lead into a discussion on how different words can have various meanings. From this, explain that the words "accuracy" and "precision" have very different definitions in the study of sciences.

Activity 11   Visualizing sound waves

In this activity students will place a fluid or light powder over a speaker to visualize the movement of the speaker and therefore study visible sound and vibrations (cymatics).

As with Activity 10, there is very little to write up for this activity. Make sure the students are sketching the patterns of sound waves throughout the experiment.

In Part A, at a certain frequency and amplitude (loudness) you see a standing wave pattern of lines, squares or hexagons on the surface of the liquid (Faraday waves). These are mathematically very complex, but are caused by interference of waves crossing the liquid's surface. In addition, at certain amplitudes (corresponding to certain accelerations of the corn starch) the sound waves passing through the corn starch liquid force the colloidal particles together and in that instant the corn starch becomes solid, forming more chaotic, vertical finger-like protrusions. It works best at low frequencies (around 100 Hz).

In Part B, the very light salt particles arrange themselves into Chladni patterns, collecting at the stationary nodes of the flat plate. Standing waves form in the plate due to reflections from the circular boundary. Changing the vibration frequency should change the positions of the nodes, resulting in a new pattern. After the experiment, students can compare their patterns of what they saw to the ones created with the metal sheet (different objects/materials have a different natural frequency or harmonic; each frequency is associated with a standing wave pattern).

Summary

Patterns can be identified by investigation or systematic classification of observable properties. Throughout this chapter, activities have provided students with opportunities to identify patterns and create their own systems of classification. Students should be aware of how to design experiments to test their predictions as a result of the patterns they have identified, and thus use patterns to further their knowledge and understanding. They should also be able to evaluate the methods used to identify patterns and consequently reflect on the accuracy and precision of their data.

Environment

	ATL skills	Science skills
TOPIC 1 Plant responses		
Activity 1 Stem response to simulated wind	✓ Make guesses, ask "what if" questions and generate testable hypotheses.	✓ Formulate a testable hypothesis and explain it using scientific reasoning. ✓ Design a method for testing a hypothesis, and select appropriate materials and equipment. ✓ Explain how to manipulate the variables and how data will be collected.
Activity 2 Responses to light	✓ Interpret data.	✓ Interpret data gained from scientific investigations and explain the results using scientific reasoning. ✓ Discuss how well the data supports a conclusion.
Activity 3 Competition	✓ Draw reasonable conclusions and generalizations.	✓ Process data and present it in an appropriate graph so that conclusions can be drawn. ✓ Interpret data gained from scientific investigations and explain the results using scientific reasoning.
TOPIC 2 Gravitational force		
Activity 4 The relationship between mass and gravity in the universe	✓ Encourage others to contribute.	✓ Draw sketches of observations from an experiment.
Activity 5 Measuring the acceleration due to gravity	✓ Process data and report results.	✓ Design a method for testing a hypothesis, and select appropriate materials and equipment. ✓ Explain how to manipulate the variables and how data will be collected. ✓ Process data and present it in an appropriate graph so that conclusions can be drawn. ✓ Interpret data gained from scientific investigations and explain the results using scientific reasoning.

Introducing environment

In both physics and biology, the word "environment" refers to the components of a defined system and their interactions. These components can be living or non-living. By studying each component in isolation and within its system, we can understand how all components are interdependent.

In this chapter, students will learn that environments can vary in size and that humans define the parameters of each environment, and thus which components we have the possibility of investigating. Both living and non-living components can simultaneously be in many different environments. By experimentation and modelling, we are able to dissect the interactions of the components within a given environment to further our understanding of scientific phenomena.

TOPIC 1   Plant responses

In this topic, students will look at relationships in the environment and how organisms respond to changes in the environment. They will investigate the effect of mechanical stress or contact on plant growth, how position affects the size of lichen patches, environmental factors affecting leaf size and shape and how competition between seedlings affects their above-ground biomass.

Students will develop their skills in formulating a testable hypothesis, interpreting data and explaining results using correct scientific reasoning.

👤 Activity 1   Stem response to simulated wind

Stage 1 of the unit planner

Key concept	Related concept(s)	Global context
Relationships	Environment Form	Scientific and technical innovation
Statement of inquiry		
Understanding a plant's relationship with its environment can help us improve plant growth and so maximize crop yields.		

This activity further explores thigmotropism, the effect of mechanical stress or contact on plant growth. The environment often contains factors that stress plants in this way.

Some possible dependent variables include stem thickness, plant height and plant above-ground biomass. The independent variable can be the frequency of mechanical stimulation.

In this experiment, the wind can be a source of mechanical stress but it can also affect water loss, which leads to stomata closure and decreased rates of photosynthesis.

🔗 CHAPTER LINKS
Activity 3 from Chapter 12 explored the effect of thigmotropism on the *Mimosa* plant.

🔗 WEB LINKS
An example of a similar experiment for a sample of papaya plants, monitored over three weeks, is described at http://hortsci.ashspublications.org/content/46/8/1105.full.pdf.

One group (squares plotted on the graph) was exposed to wind and the other was shielded from wind (triangles). Differences in stem height and root tip density were measured. Students can be asked to analyse the data to draw the conclusion that wind appears to affect stem height and root tip density.

The experiment suggested in the student book considers just mechanical stress. The expected results are not clear as mechanical stress might even improve plant growth outcomes.

Assessment

If you choose to assess students on this task, you can use criterion B or C. The task-specific descriptor in the top band (7–8) should read that students are able to:

WEB LINKS

This gardener's website suggests stressing tomato plants mechanically to give improved growth outcomes: www.veggiegardeningtips.com/happy-tomato-plants.

Criterion B

- explain that they are trying to measure the effect of mechanical stress on plant growth
- formulate and explain a testable hypothesis involving a variable that might affect the stem thickness, plant height or above-ground biomass, using correct scientific reasoning
- explain how to manipulate and control the variables, and how sufficient, relevant data will be collected; for example, explaining why at least five values of the independent variable will be tested, why repeat measurements will increase confidence in the conclusion, and how other factors will be controlled
- design a logical, complete and safe method in which they select appropriate materials and equipment, including how the dependent variable chosen will be measured.

Criterion C

- correctly organize results in a suitable table, process data (calculating mean of repeat readings) and correctly present processed data as a scatter graph with a line of best fit
- accurately interpret data, identifying a relationship from the graph, and explain results using correct scientific reasoning
- evaluate the validity of the hypothesis based on the outcome of their scientific investigation
- evaluate the validity of the method based on conditions of the experiment, fair testing procedure and whether enough data was collected to address the question
- explain improvements or extensions to the method, and explain how they could reduce sources of error and give more accurate results.

Activity 2   Responses to light

This activity looks at how the environment of a lichen influences its growth.

Answers

a) The data appears to support the conclusion that there is a difference in patch size on the top and on the side of walls, as the mean of the top group is 19.8 mm and the mean of the side group is 13 mm.
b) The data is highly variable, and the two data sets differ in the degree to which they vary. The sample size is small and therefore might not be a representative sample of the population of lichens.

Further exploration

If supported by the school's maths curriculum, students might refer to the fact that the standard deviation of the two data sets is high and differs between the two groups.

Activity 3   Competition

This activity looks at how individuals of the same species compete for resources.

[SAFETY]

Students should always wash their hands after handling the soil and seeds. Whatever seeds are used, they should not be pre-treated with pesticides.

You can ask students to consider why it is necessary, as given in the instructions, to space the seeds in a regular pattern; to rotate the pots at regular intervals; to grow the plants for one week after the appearance of true leaves; and to determine both the total biomass for the pot and the mean biomass of each plant.

TOPIC 2   Gravitational force

WEB LINKS

For a description of the gravitational pull of Earth in relation to satellites, go to www.s-cool.co.uk/gcse and click on "physics", "space", and then "the solar system".

This topic links well with activities in Chapter 12 on movement (which relates to Newton's laws of motion) and with Chapter 4 on relationships (which uses Newton's law of universal gravitation as an example of mathematical relationship).

Students will gain a deeper understanding of the gravitational force between two masses, and carry out a simple demonstration to visualize this as a warping of space–time.

They will then determine the acceleration due to gravity in an inquiry-based experiment. They will move on to discussing the space debris that is currently orbiting the Earth and how it affects our spatial environment. They will gain a deep understanding of gravity, which is fundamental to our lives.

TEACHING IDEA 1

To introduce this topic, you can show the students a video demonstrating a satellite launch.

Search for one on You Tube and then a discussion can follow on how students think the satellite stays in space (the pull of gravity from the Earth).

Activity 4   The relationship between mass and gravity in the universe

In this activity, students will gain insight into the relationship between mass and gravity. This activity should demonstrate to students how massive bodies in space affect the motion of other bodies. The basketball represents a mass in space similar to a star, and the tennis ball represents a smaller mass such as a planet.

By visualizing the gravitational force between the two masses as a warping (distortion) of the space–time "fabric" around them, students will gain a basic understanding of Einstein's theory.

You can ask students to bring in bedsheets; alternatively, they can use lab coats in smaller groups.

Students should learn that space–time is warped by the presence of mass. They should notice that in the presence of mass, the moving tennis ball bends its path towards the mass.

TIP

Try to avoid saying "the ball rolls *down* into the hole"—this is invoking gravity to explain gravity. Stick to saying that the path is distorted from a straight line—remember, looking at it from the other side, the ball appears to climb out of the hole.

Further exploration

Students can research Albert Einstein's theory of general relativity and how it differs from Isaac Newton's law of universal gravitation. A further activity could be to research if, in theory, time travel is possible. If students complete this, they can present their ideas to the class.

 Activity 5 Measuring the acceleration due to gravity

Stage 1 of the unit planner

Key concept	Related concept(s)	Global context
Relationships	Environment Movement	Identities and relationships
Statement of inquiry		
Understanding our relationship with our environment has helped us gain a better understanding of space.		

This activity will help students gain a deeper understanding of gravity, which they can link to the topic of satellites orbiting Earth. They need to understand (a) that gravity is a force that causes masses to accelerate, and (b) that acceleration is the rate of change of velocity with units m/s². Do not give students the value of acceleration due to gravity as this is what they are trying to find.

Students must come up with their own inquiry question and method, using the apparatus listed in the student book. The prompt questions in the student book should help them achieve this. Their method should not assume that the acceleration is constant—that is, they should not use equations for constant acceleration such as:

$$s = \frac{1}{2} g t^2$$

Assessment

If you choose to assess students on this task, you can use criterion B or C. The task-specific descriptor in the top band (7–8) should read that students are able to:

Criterion B

- explain that they are trying to measure the acceleration due to gravity
- formulate and explain a testable hypothesis involving variables that might affect the acceleration due to gravity, using correct scientific reasoning
- explain how to manipulate and control the variables, measuring variables accurately and checking reproducibility of results, and explain how sufficient, relevant data will be collected to find the acceleration due to gravity
- design a logical, complete and safe method in which they select appropriate materials and equipment to find the acceleration due to gravity.

Criterion C

- correctly organize results in a suitable table, process data (calculating mean of repeat readings) and correctly present processed data as a scatter graph with a line of best fit

TIP

If students are struggling to formulate an inquiry question, you can help by prompting them to pick variables to manipulate and decide which variable must be controlled. For example, does the acceleration due to gravity vary with the height from which the mass falls, or with the mass of the object? Students will also need to decide what variables are needed to describe the motion of a falling mass (time, distance fallen, speed) and hence how they will calculate the acceleration.

CHAPTER LINKS

It is useful if students have completed Activities 8 and 9 in Chapter 12 on movement before attempting this activity, so that they are familiar with the ticker tape apparatus for measuring speed and acceleration.

WEB LINKS

A further method of finding the acceleration due to gravity with an electronic timer uses an electromagnetic release mechanism. However, this method, investigating the relationship between velocity and height fallen, assumes constant acceleration.

Go to:
http://www.nuffieldfoundation.org/practical-physics and search for "acceleration due to gravity".

- accurately interpret data, identifying a relationship from the graph, and explain results using correct scientific reasoning
- evaluate the validity of the hypothesis based on the outcome of their scientific investigation
- evaluate the validity of the method based on conditions of the experiment, fair testing procedure and whether enough data was collected to address the question
- explain improvements or extensions to the method that would benefit finding acceleration due to gravity, and explain how they could reduce sources of error and give more accurate results.

QUICK THINK

It would be good for the students to research the debris in space (non-functional satellites, debris from fragmentation of objects put into orbit) and the implications of having no operational satellites. Students should specifically research the Kessler syndrome (cascading collisions) and how it could affect our environment. The blockbuster movie *Gravity* uses this scenario. Students should also include the current procedures in place to prevent the creation of new fragments, and to remove debris from space. The following links should help students complete this activity:

www.spacesafetymagazine.com/space-debris/kessler-syndrome/

www.theguardian.com/science/blog/2013/nov/15/space-junk-apocalypse-gravity

www.fromquarkstoquasars.com/the-seriousness-of-the-kessler-syndrome/

QUICK THINK

Students will need to understand how the Juno spacecraft, launched in 2011, was pulled back towards the Sun in its 2-year heliocentric orbit. Then, as it came close to Earth again in October 2013, it was pulled into the Earth's gravitational field. This boosted the spacecraft's velocity relative to the Sun (without using fuel), enabling it to overcome the Sun's gravitational field and fling itself further out into the Solar System on a trajectory to Jupiter, its final destination. The gravity assist manoeuvre reduces the amount of rocket fuel required by a launch vehicle. The instruments on Juno will measure the amount of atmospheric water and ammonia in Jupiter's deep atmosphere and investigate its magnetic field to help us learn more about the creation of the Solar System.

 **WEB LINKS**
You can find some additional resources describing the mission here: www.nasa.gov/mission_pages/juno/main/#.VCu2wfldV0E

Summary

As students progressed through this chapter, they studied the interactions of components within different environments. Students should understand that the different aspects of a system do not exist in isolation, and that by creating models of each environment, we are able to test theories about the different interactions that we observe in the natural world and via experimentation. This chapter focuses on designing experiments that facilitate the investigation of specific interactions within a given environment, enabling students to gather and organize information, draw reasonable conclusions to form arguments and evaluate models of systems.

		ATL skills	Science skills
TOPIC 1 Balance in biology			
	Activity 1 Exploring thermoregulation	✓ Gather and organize relevant information to formulate an argument.	✓ Draw conclusions, and explain these using scientific reasoning.
	Activity 2 Interpreting data regarding the diving reflex	✓ Interpret data.	✓ Analyse data to draw justifiable conclusions.
	Activity 3 The diving reflex in humans	✓ Make guesses, ask "what if" questions and generate testable hypotheses.	✓ Formulate a testable hypothesis. ✓ Design a method and select appropriate materials and equipment. ✓ Explain how to manipulate variables, and how enough data will be collected.
	Activity 4 Balance in a pond community	✓ Draw reasonable conclusions and generalizations.	✓ Draw conclusions, and explain these using scientific reasoning.
TOPIC 2 Balance in chemical reactions			
	Activity 5 Dealing with very large amounts— the mole	✓ Understand and use mathematical notation.	✓ Solve problems set in unfamiliar situations.
	Activity 6 Determining the formula of a hydrate	✓ Process data and report results.	✓ Organize and present data in tables ready for processing. ✓ Analyse data to draw justifiable conclusions.

Introducing balance

Balance refers to a stable equilibrium whereby measurable variables are constant over time or fluctuate around a constant within limited parameters. In biology, the equilibrium is dynamic and reflects constant change as a result of interactions between living organisms and their environment. In chemistry, mathematics is used to describe equilibria and facilitate the modelling of chemical reactions. Chemists can then use these equations to predict the required reactants or expected products of chemical reactions.

In this chapter, students will investigate how balance is maintained in biological systems and in chemical reactions. Students will explore how biological organisms remain balanced over time, in terms of their internal environment and of their interaction with their environment. Students will also use mathematics and chemical models of balance to formulate and test hypotheses about chemical reactions.

TOPIC 1 Balance in biology

In this topic, students will look at the mechanisms that living things possess to maintain balance, including homeostasis and the balance that exists in stable ecosystems. They will explore thermoregulation following disruptions to body temperature, the diving reflex in humans—for example, how heart rate is affected by holding your breath—and balance in a stable pond community.

Students will develop their skills in designing an experiment, forming and testing a hypothesis, making predictions and interpreting data.

 Activity 1 **Exploring thermoregulation**

This activity looks at skin surface temperature and explores thermoregulation.

[SAFETY]

Since this activity requires students to put ice cubes in their mouth, it is best to perform the experiment away from the science lab, since there is a slight risk of contamination. The activity can be carried out in a classroom or, even better, in a food/cookery room using ice trays from a food fridge rather than a science fridge. Care should be taken not to injure students' skin by exposure to ice.

Further exploration

Further explorations in thermoregulation can include comparing how long it takes ice-cooled skin to return to a baseline temperature on different parts of the body, such as the cheek or the arm. These areas differ in the degree of vascularization and so should recover at different rates.

Activity 2   Interpreting data regarding the diving reflex

This activity looks at the heart rate of an elephant seal and its corresponding dive depth, and requires students to analyse and interpret the data.

Answers

a) The number of dives that occurred between 12:00 and 18:00: 21–23.

b) Longer, less frequent dives in the early afternoon; shorter, more frequent dives in the later afternoon.

c) The deepest dive taken by the elephant seal was approximately 485 metres.

d) The longest dive taken by the elephant seal was approximately 30 minutes.

e) Whenever the seal dives, heart rate is suppressed; in shorter, shallower dives, the heart rate does not go as low.

 Activity 3   The diving reflex in humans

This activity requires students to design an investigation related to the diving reflex in humans.

Possible questions include:

a) Is heart rate affected by holding your breath?

b) Is heart rate affected by putting a cold pack on your cheek? (immersing your face in cold water?)

c) Is heart rate affected by putting a warm pack on your cheek? (immersing your face in warm water?)

d) Could a person with their face immersed in cold water hold their breath longer than a person with their face immersed in warm water?

The equipment needed includes bowls of tap water, ice, cold and warm packs and thermometers. Pulse rate can be measured manually at the wrist with a stopwatch, or using a heart rate monitor. Students should suggest calculating the percentage change from resting pulse rate in response to each test condition.

[SAFETY]

Experiments to immerse the face in water should **not** be carried out, just hypothesised, as it requires parental consent and, in any event, should not be carried out in a laboratory due to the risk of chemical contamination from the sink or bowl. If you plan to allow students to carry out an investigation related to questions (a), (b) and (c) above, ask students to inform you if they have heart or breathing problems (such as asthma) before attempting the activities. Students should not attempt to hold their breath for longer than is comfortable.

Care should be taken not to injure students' skin by exposure to ice or the cold and warm packs.

Inform students that their participation as experimental subjects is voluntary and that they can withdraw at any time.

Before doing this activity, students need a basic understanding of the human cardiovascular and respiratory systems.

If they were to be carried out, the heart rate activities would show that slowed pulse rate (the diving reflex) is not observed during normal breath-holding in air or when the face is placed in warm water. Heart rate would actually increase in these two conditions.

Discuss the physiological significance of the experiment: an automatic reflex to slow heart rate reduces blood flow to organs where it is not needed and so prioritizes blood flow to the brain and heart; this conserves oxygen and extends the amount of time a person can stay under water. The diving reflex is much better developed in seals and whales, which can stay under water for 20 minutes to an hour.

Further exploration

Students could explore where the sensory receptors on the face are (the forehead, nose or cheeks) and, for example, whether exposure of the forehead to cold water is essential for the diving response.

Activity 4 **Balance in a pond community**

In this experiment, the removal of larger organisms will be verified. Students can be encouraged to investigate whether there is a correlation between size and trophic level. Students can verify the extent to which these organisms are removed using a microscope or hand lens. It is likely that, at a minimum, the initial filtering will reduce the number and diversity of organisms in the system.

Removing primary consumers should increase the amount of plant and algae biomass in the jar, which would result in greater amounts of bubbling initially but may lead to an increase in detritus at the base of the jar.

Removing secondary consumers may result in a decrease in plant biomass as a lack of predation on primary consumers results, in turn, in an increase in predation on the producers. Reducing tertiary consumers would result in a proliferation of organisms from other trophic levels.

[SAFETY]

Water samples must not be taken from sources likely to contain faecal or sewage pollution. Beware of *Leptospira* contamination of pond water, which causes Weil's disease. Do not keep the water samples above 25 °C. Ensure students cover cuts or abrasions with waterproof plasters or gloves before handling pond water. Students should also wash their hands with antibacterial soap after handling pond water and disinfect the work area both before the investigation and afterwards.

Further exploration

Students could also conduct experiments regarding the effect on balance of altering light entry, enriching with nutrients, changing the amount of air in the closed container or allowing the exchange of matter with the surroundings.

TIP

The beakers of pond water should be placed in a well-lit area and monitored. As the experiment progresses, these ecosystem models can give off a bad smell, depending on the pond water source. The cover over the system is important. Rather than take samples, students can make a visual inspection of the differences.

TOPIC 2 Balance in chemical reactions

The related concept of balance is at the heart of chemistry; this is what allows chemistry to change from purely a qualitative science to a quantitative science. Teaching this topic will enable students to understand that a central idea of stoichiometry is the law of conservation of mass. From this law comes the idea of balancing equations, and relating amounts of reactants and products in a reaction.

TEACHING IDEA 1
Ask students to research the concept of balance in their everyday lives and then relate it to the law of conservation of mass. How are they similar? How are they different? Students could illustrate their research in a poster, a journal article, a blog post, song lyrics or a photo collage.

In this topic, students will focus on the related concept of balance. Introduction of the idea of mass and moles will eventually lead them to the study of stoichiometry. Students will observe two demonstrations that will challenge their thoughts; practise balancing equations; learn about the mole and molar mass; and determine the formula of a hydrate.

Before students examine more closely the concept of balance, they should review their knowledge of writing chemical formulae, naming chemicals and performing calculations involving percentages.

Activity 5 — Dealing with very large amounts—the mole

In this activity, students become familiar with simple calculations surrounding the idea of moles—a way of representing a very large amount. Because atomic particles are so small, chemists had to come up with a way of representing extremely large amounts of something. Even a single drop of water contains 1.67×10^{21} molecules; imagine how many water drops fill a swimming pool, or a lake or the Indian Ocean.

You can use any five substances that you wish in any amount that will fit in a plastic bag and can be measured with the balances that are available. You may wish to plan to use more inert chemicals in case the bags are tampered with. Ensure that the substances that you provide in step 5 are all elements. You will want to ensure that students provide evidence of their calculations in addition to a data table.

Students should complete a table like the following to record their observations.

DP LINKS
This activity links with DP chemistry Topic 8 where students will further investigate the properties of acids and bases, and further examine the function of indicators.

WEB LINKS
In order for students to get the formulae for compounds listed on food labels, they can use this website: www.endmemo.com/chem/chemsearch.php

TIP

Care should be taken to ensure that the plastic bags are not pierced or punctured.

Compound name	Chemical formula	Mass (g)	Number of moles	Number of molecules
Zinc	Zn		1.50	
Glucose				6.02×10^{21}
Sample				

Activity 6 Determining the formula of a hydrate

The hydrates used in this activity will depend on what is available in your chemical store cupboard. Common hydrates to use in this activity include copper(II) sulfate pentahydrate, cobalt(II) chloride dihydrate and manganese(II) sulfate tetrahydrate. It is suggested that the heat source used for this activity is a Bunsen burner. If you modify your heat source, you may have to modify the procedure so that you use an evaporating dish on a hot plate. You may want to do a quick review of percentage calculations so that students are familiar with this idea. Provide students with the list of possible hydrate formulae. Students should be directed to use approximately 4 g of hydrate.

Students are to first calculate the percentage of water in each possible hydrate:

$$\% \text{ by mass of water in hydrate} = \frac{\text{total molar mass of water}}{\text{total molar mass of water}} \times 100$$

The data that students need to collect should be displayed in a sample data table.

Measurement	Mass (g)
mass of clean dry test tube	
mass of clean dry test tube + hydrate sample	
mass of hydrate (calculated)	
mass of test tube + hydrate after first heating	
mass of test tube + hydrate after second heating	
mass of anhydrous salt remaining (calculated)	
mass of water lost (calculated)	
% by mass of water in hydrate (calculated)	
identity of unknown hydrate	

Possible sources of error in this experiment include:

- some water may have evaporated from the substance during storage
- additional water molecules may have been added to the substance during storage
- the substance was not heated long enough; not all the water has evaporated from the hydrate
- the substance was heated too long; a chemical reaction occurred that would have changed the mass and composition of the anhydrous salt.

[SAFETY]
Students should wear eye protection, heat the hydrate over a gentle heat and stop heating when the sample has lost all its water.

Summary

In this chapter, students have learned that there are many different mechanisms that require a balanced system. They investigated how biological systems require the maintenance of balance in order to survive, and the stability provided by dynamic equilibria enables life to thrive. Students should now be able to predict how organisms will respond to a change in their internal or external environment in order to maintain this balance. They have also practised using mathematics to describe chemical reactions and apply their knowledge of balance to predict and measure the outcomes of these reactions.